Sophocles' Antigone

Sophocles' *Antigone* comes alive in this new translation that will be useful for both academic study and stage production. Diane J. Rayor's accurate yet accessible translation reflects the play's inherent theatricality. She provides an analytical introduction and comprehensive notes, and the edition includes an essay by director Karen Libman.

Antigone begins after Oedipus and Jocasta's sons have killed each other in a battle over the kingship. The new king, Kreon, decrees that the brother who attacked with a foreign army remain unburied and promises death to anyone who defies him. The play centers on Antigone's refusal to obey Kreon's law and Kreon's refusal to allow her brother's burial. Each acts on principle colored by gender, personality, and family history. *Antigone* poses a conflict between passionate characters whose extreme stances leave no room for compromise. The highly charged struggle between the individual person and the state has powerful implications for ethical and political situations today.

DIANE J. RAYOR is Professor of Classics at Grand Valley State University in Michigan. She has published three book-length translations of ancient Greek poetry: *Homeric Hymns: A Translation, with Introduction and Notes* (2004); *Sappho's Lyre: Archaic Lyric and Women Poets of Ancient Greece* (1991), winner of the Columbia University Translation Center Merit Award in 1992; and, with Stanley Lombardo, *Callimachus* (1988). She also co-edited *Latin Lyric and Elegiac Poetry* (1995), and her translations appear in numerous anthologies.

Sophocles' Antigone

A New Translation

Translated and Edited by
DIANE J. RAYOR
Grand Valley State University, Michigan

With Director's Note by
KAREN LIBMAN

CAMBRIDGE
UNIVERSITY PRESS

32 Avenue of the Americas, New York NY 10013-2473, USA

Cambridge University Press is part of the University of Cambridge.

It furthers the University's mission by disseminating knowledge in the pursuit of education, learning and research at the highest international levels of excellence.

www.cambridge.org
Information on this title: www.cambridge.org/9780521134781

First published 2011

A catalogue record for this publication is available from the British Library

Library of Congress Cataloguing in Publication data

Sophocles.
[Antigone. English]
Antigone : a new translation / [Sophocles] ; translated and edited by Diane J. Rayor.
   p. cm.
Includes bibliographical references and index.
ISBN 978-0-521-11928-3 – ISBN 978-0-521-13478-1 (pbk.)
1. Antigone (Greek mythology) – Drama.   I. Rayor, Diane J.   II. Title.
PA4414.A7R39   2011
882'.01–dc22   2010046927

ISBN 978-0-521-11928-3 Hardback
ISBN 978-0-521-13478-1 Paperback

For Connie and Harold Rayor,
and Adele and Malcolm Hast,
with love and gratitude.

Contents

Acknowledgments
ix

Introduction
xi

Scene List
xxv

Cast of Characters
xxvii

ANTIGONE
I

Note from a Stage Director by Karen Libman
65

Notes
69

Selected Bibliography
93

Acknowledgments

Although my usual method of translation depends on many willing readers and listeners, drama calls for a larger cast.

In the 2008 Paros Symposium of Conversation and Translation in Greece, I worked extensively on the first and third choral odes with poets Susan Gevirtz, Vassilis Manoussakis, and Angelos Sakkis. I gratefully acknowledge Susan Gevirtz for inviting me and helping me develop a choral voice during the week-long workshop, Grand Valley State University (GVSU) for my travel funding, and the European Center for the Translation of Literature and the Human Sciences (EKEMEL) for providing my accommodations in Paros.

I am thankful for my students' participation in the development of this book, beginning and ending with those in my advanced Greek classes in 2008 (April Conant, Hannah Gaff, Brittany Hunter, Benjamin Sparks, and Devin White) and 2010 (Mark Beckwith, Jennifer Folkerth, Lauren Janicki, Donna St. Louis, and Shannon S. Schupbach). I also want to thank the students in my mythology, classical world, literary translation, and ancient religion courses (2008–10).

The most extensive revisions occurred in the semester rehearsal and production (April 2009) of the GVSU Classical Theatre Workshop, under the vibrant direction of Karen Libman; the talented cast and director helped me see and hear every line and so helped shape the translation and supplementary material. Special thanks go to Evin Anderson, Nicholas Law, and Aaron Sohaski.

A second production of this translation (November 2009) was beautifully staged by theater director Todd Avery and his Jenison High School cast, and it provided another opportunity for me to answer questions and fine-tune the translation for performance.

My profound gratitude goes to my family of editors: Connie Rayor, Janet Rayor, Daniel Rayor Hast, and David Hast (whose steady support makes my work possible). Long ago, when we were about Antigone and Ismene's age, my sister Linda and I played those parts.

This *Antigone* was initiated by and concludes under the thoughtful care of Beatrice Rehl and Cambridge University Press. I am grateful to the three anonymous referees whose valuable critiques influenced the direction of the translation. I especially thank Ruth Scodel for her meticulous criticism, which greatly improved the final product; she bears no responsibility for errors I persist in.

Introduction

Sophocles' *Antigone* is the most read and performed of all Greek tragedies. The play poses a conflict between passionate characters whose extreme stances leave no room for compromise or diplomacy. Antigone's character may also represent the rights of the individual, family, and women and the authority of traditional customs, in opposition to Kreon's representation of the law, the state, male authority, and political institutions. In addition, the important role and responsibility of the community (the chorus of elders) run as undercurrents throughout. The powerful conflict of principles in *Antigone* makes it highly adaptable to modern ethical dilemmas and political situations.[1]

GREEK TRAGEDY

Festival to Dionysos

Greek tragedy was composed for performance at an annual Athenian festival honoring the god Dionysos. That festival, called the Great

---

[1] See Steiner (1986), Mackay (1989), and Nelli (2009).

Dionysia or City Dionysia, became fully integrated into the new Athenian democracy in the fifth century BCE. Athenian playwrights wrote and directed all of the plays for a primarily Athenian audience of 15,000–20,000 that gathered together for a six-day festival in an act of citizenship and community.[2]

In addition to being a political event celebrating Athenian democracy and imperial power, the City Dionysia was a religious ceremony dedicated to the worship of Dionysos, the god of theater, ecstasy, inspiration, vegetation, wine, and dithyrambic (cult) song. Dionysian dithyramb involved song, dance, masks, and costume – all major components of Greek theater.

Organization and Funding

The dramatic competition was state organized and supported, with plays designed for a single performance at the City Dionysia. Playwrights applied in mid-summer for inclusion in the festival to be held the following March. The annual state official selected three playwrights, each of whom entered three tragedies and one shorter satyr play that provided some comic relief after the tragedies.[3] The three tragedies could be a unified trilogy, like Aeschylus' *Oresteia*, followed by a thematically connected satyr play, or they could be entirely separate plays. For three days beginning at dawn the audiences watched plays, with one tragedian presenting each day.[4] At the

---

[2] In Aristophanes' comedy *Frogs*, Euripides claims that tragic poets should be respected because "we make people in cities better" (1009–10); that is, better citizens.

[3] Satyrs – bawdy male creatures depicted with pointy ears, horse tails, and erect phalluses – were associated with Dionysos in myth.

[4] Early on, a comedy was performed in the late afternoons; later, a separate day was added for comedy.

end of the competition, a panel of ten judges ranked tragedians for their four plays and awarded a prize for the best production.

To fund dramatic productions and other expensive projects considered vital to the state, a special "liturgy" tax was imposed on wealthy citizens. The liturgies could fund warships or various public works or support and costume a chorus during its six-month rehearsal period. The wealthy patrons, who could choose which projects to fund, covered all the expenses involving the chorus, whereas the state paid for the costs of at least one of the actors.[5]

Dramatists

The three playwrights of tragedy whose plays survive are Aeschylus (c. 525–456 BCE), Sophocles (c. 496–406 BCE), and Euripides (485–406 BCE). Each wrote 80–120 tragedies, yet only 32 survive. In the fourth century BCE, some of the plays were performed again, so copies must have been available then. Sophocles was said never to have come in third in the competitions, and even though we know of 118 titles of plays by Sophocles, only 7 of his plays survive.[6]

Theater Conventions

The plays were performed in the theater of Dionysos on the southern slope of the hill below the Akropolis and near the temple of Dionysos. The theater consisted of tiers of benches for the audience (viewing place/*theatron*) arranged in a semi-circle around the circular dancing place at ground level for the chorus (*orchestra*), two side paths (*parodoi*) leading into the orchestra, and the scene building

---

[5] Ley (2006) 9.
[6] Scodel (1984b) 8; an excellent introduction to Sophocles.

(*skenê*) with central double doors, which was located at the back of the orchestra.[7] The *skenê* allowed actors to make entrances and exits, provided room for costume changes, and could represent a house, palace, or any interior space. Actors and the chorus also entered or exited on the side paths; each *parodos* could represent a different destination. In *Antigone*, one path leads to the city (CP) and the other to the burial place or battlefield (BP). Although the scripts mention some properties, sets and props were minimal, and the visible spectacle of the chorus and the power of language carried the play. The all-male chorus and actors wore long, colorful robes and full head masks with wigs.

Choral performances, an ancient genre long predating drama, formed the initial core of dramas. Sophocles increased the chorus from twelve to fifteen members, who sang and danced to the accompaniment of an *aulos* (double-reed pipe) and percussion. At some point before the fifth century, the playwright became the first actor, speaking to the chorus and possibly the audience. Aeschylus was credited with adding a second actor, and Sophocles a third. Thereafter, the use of three speaking actors became standard practice, although there could be silent extras and children with limited or no lines. Because the three actors wore masks, they could play multiple characters. Eventually, perhaps with the increased complexity of directing more actors and of acting roles that included song, the playwright continued to direct but no longer acted in his own plays. Even though the acoustics in Greek theaters are excellent, the actors and chorus would need very strong voices to carry them through the four plays all performed in a single day. Masks and large audiences negated any effect of facial expressions or small gestures. Scripts were not circulated widely in the primarily oral society, so audiences would be attuned to remembering spoken or sung verse.

[7] Ley (2006) 17–20.

Meter

In the original Greek, the plays are entirely in verse, with spoken lines primarily in iambic, choral songs in complex lyric meters, and chanted portions in anapests. The chorus, with the force of communal authority, sings in unison the complex lyric songs between scenes. In general, actors speak and choruses sing. During highly emotional scenes, however, an actor may break out in song, directed to the chorus in a lament or *kommos*. *Antigone* contains two such episodes: Antigone's final march to her death and Kreon's final scene. In brief dialogue with actors within a scene, the chorus leader generally does not sing but speaks in the same meter as the actors.

The chorus leader also sometimes chants, either at the end of a choral ode or within a scene, because scripts record almost no stage directions, which are usually cued in the dialogue itself.[8] The chorus in *Antigone* announces most entrances and exits. The anapestic meter, probably chanted by the chorus leader, introduces a character's entrance in the last stanza of the first four choral odes and within a few scenes.

The Play Structure

Scenes alternate with choral odes, which provide a hinge[9] between two scenes. The chorus comments on the previous scene and introduces or sets the stage for the next one. During scenes, the chorus leader speaks briefly for the chorus, and his/their response can change the course of events. Although the chorus rarely takes action itself, they can question, advise, and urge characters to action. They tend to present the voice of the community within the play. Characters often deliver

[8] Taplin (2003).
[9] Goldhill (2007) 50.

lengthy, virtuoso speeches alternating with rapid, impassioned, primarily single-line dialogue (*stichomythia*). Messengers also give long speeches, which report offstage action, especially violent action.[10]

Play Topics

With one exception (Aeschylus' *Persians*), the tragedies drew from the mythological past rather than current events. Homer's *Iliad* and *Odyssey*, other epics, and lyric poetry provided the tragedians with many versions of popular stories from which to choose. For instance, the late-seventh-century lyric poet Stesichoros is a source for Euripides' *Helen* in which Helen never goes to Troy;[11] the gods create a phantom Helen whom Paris kidnaps, while the real Helen remains chastely trapped in Egypt. Many dramatists used different versions of the same subject matter – witness the three extant Electra plays – and were free to create their own variants. Many works explored the Theban house of Laius, with events differing from Sophocles' extant versions (Jocasta does not hang herself, Haemon dies before Antigone's birth, Haemon and Antigone have a son, or Antigone and Ismene die in a fire). Although today editions of the three plays are often bundled as a trilogy, Sophocles wrote *Antigone* first (probably in the late 440s BCE), *Oedipus Tyrannos* perhaps twenty years later (420s?), and *Oedipus at Kolonos* was produced posthumously in 401 BCE. The two other extant versions of the Theban cycle are Aeschylus' *Seven against Thebes* and Euripides' *Phoenician Women*. The characters and details in each of these Theban plays should be considered separately rather than as fitting tidily into a single narrative.

[10] Goldhill (2007) 81ff. notes chorus, *stichomythia*, and messenger speeches as most problematic for modern performances.

[11] Rayor (1991) 39, Stesichoros PMG 192: "This story is not true, / you did not sail in full-decked ships / nor reach the towers of Troy."

The dramas concern royal houses mostly located outside of the Athenian territory of Attica. Athens is spared in most tragedies, and bad things, such as incest and murders within the family, tend to happen elsewhere, usually in rival states such as Thebes or Korinth. Locating the stories in other places and in a distant past provides a psychological distance that enables all the participants (audience and dramatists) to explore and question vital ethical issues. Greek tragedy serves a similar function for us today.[12]

Sophocles' *Antigone*

Sophocles of Kolonos (an Athenian district) won his first of eighteen to twenty-four victories at the Dionysia in 468 BCE. In addition to being a favored and prolific composer, he was associated with the Athenian worship of the healer god Asklepios and served in various religious and military positions, including as treasurer (443/2 BCE) and general in a war against Samos (441/40 BCE).[13]

Mythic Background

Laius, son of Labdacus, left his infant son Oedipus to die because of a prophecy that Oedipus was fated to kill him. After being raised

---

[12] Nelli (2009) 72: "It seems that when the dictatorship was finally over, writers and directors not only realized that the play [*Antigone*] had many things to say about the repression suffered by the people but also that, due to the remoteness of its plot in terms of time and place, it possessed a much more powerful way of expressing and effectively communicating them to an Argentine audience. It was easier to reflect on the recent events by 'showing' them as having occurred long ago and far away."

[13] Scodel (1984b) 6–7.

far from Thebes, Oedipus killed Laius, unaware that he was his father, in an act of road rage. Shortly after, he married the widowed queen Jocasta, his own mother. They had four children before they discovered the truth of their relationship. In Sophocles' *Oedipus Tyrannos* (King), Jocasta hangs herself and Oedipus blinds himself before leaving Thebes in exile. In *Oedipus at Kolonos*, Antigone, one of his four children, is her father's guide.

The *Antigone* play begins after the climactic battle in which Oedipus and Jocasta's sons, Eteokles and Polynices, kill each other while fighting over the kingship. According to other versions but not mentioned in *Antigone*, their deaths fulfill Oedipus' dying curse that his sons either destroy Thebes or each other. In some versions, Eteokles and Polynices were to alternate in ruling Thebes, but Eteokles refuses to step down after his turn. Polynices marries the king of Argos' daughter and returns with the Argive army to conquer Thebes. The night before *Antigone* begins, the brothers kill each other, the Argive army flees in defeat, and Thebes is saved. Jocasta's brother Kreon, a general in the battle, assumes the kingship as the nearest male relative left alive. For his first law as king, Kreon decrees that his nephew Polynices, as a traitor who attacked with a foreign army, must remain unburied and that anyone caught burying him be put to death. The play opens the same night, some time before dawn, with Antigone calling her sister Ismene out of the house.

The Duty of Burial

The play centers on the passionate conflict between Antigone and Kreon. Their standoff results in punishments for both: Antigone for refusing to obey Kreon's decree and Kreon for refusing to allow her brother Polynices' burial – and for burying the living Antigone instead. Both Antigone and Kreon act on stated principles colored by their personalities, gender, and family history.

The Athenian audience would have approached the play with the understanding of the importance of a proper burial and that the family's duty is to bury its dead. A proper burial allows the dead to cross over into the underworld; it protects the state and citizens from the religious and physical pollution of an exposed corpse. The Greeks' deep-seated horror of animals mutilating the body is made clear in Homer's *Iliad*[14] and later sources.

Families had the sacred responsibility to bury their dead, with men and women having distinct roles. As the closest male kin, Kreon should be the one to arrange for Polynices' burial. Women were responsible for bathing, dressing, and anointing the body and for laying it out for viewing. The body would repose on view in the courtyard of the house, while women sang ritual lamentations.[15] Men performed the burial of either the whole body or of cremated bones and ashes.

By the fifth century, the Athenian state regulated funerals both through earlier laws on general burial practices and more recent laws governing state funerals for men killed in war. Although the earlier laws aimed to curb extravagant funerary displays by the aristocracy, they also resulted in restricting women's public lamentation in the funeral procession and at the gravesite. Funeral laments had the potential to incite political disorder. The funeral for war dead ensured equality in honoring the dead and promoted civic pride. It also allotted only limited time for women to mourn privately before the dead were buried in elaborate public funerals under state control.[16]

[14] Achilles' rage made men "prey for dogs and a feast for birds" (*Iliad* 1.4–5).
[15] Bacon (1994/5).
[16] Tyrrell and Bennett (1998) 8–11.

In general, burial of the dead was a sacred obligation, particularly of kin, but traitors might be forbidden burial within the boundaries of the *polis* or city-state, which included the urban center and the surrounding rural territory. For example, Athenian traitors could be denied burial within Attica; the law forbidding burial of traitors may have been in effect as early as the production of *Antigone*.[17] However, it would be unusual to forbid everyone from burying a man *outside* of the home territory of the deceased and to post guards to enforce that decree. Why could Polynices not be buried outside of Theban territory? Kreon takes an extreme position within his legitimate authority to prevent the burial of a traitor (who is also his nephew). Kreon rules Thebes as the nearest relative of Oedipus' family, yet he repudiates familial bonds with Oedipus' children. To an Athenian audience, however, it would also be considered shocking for a woman to defy male authority boldly, without hesitation. Unlike her sister Ismene, Antigone assumes the right to transgress traditional gender boundaries. Like other tragedies, *Antigone* "explores situations in which women's loyalties to their families conflict with their appropriate social roles."[18] Yet, in the context of the play and in the absence of proper male support, Antigone's determination to bury her brother and not allow his body to be mutilated must be seen as sympathetic.[19]

Women in Athenian Society

Women in Athens were lifelong legal minors, who exercised no political or financial rights. A woman was not a legally or morally responsible agent in Athens. Respectable citizen women left home only to

[17] Holt (1999) 663.
[18] Scodel (2005) 235.
[19] Holt (1999); an excellent article on interpreting *Antigone* in scene order.

attend religious rituals and funerals and to aid in childbirth. For-
tunately, they had an active religious life and participated in the
many Athenian festivals, including dramatic festivals. The woman's
guardian (*kyrios*) – father, husband, son, or closest male relative –
would be her representative for all legal and financial decisions. Kreon
would be Antigone's *kyrios*, because her father and brothers are dead
and she is unmarried.

Marriage and Death

The Athenian *polis* consisted of a collection of individual households,
the *oikos*, which included the extended family, slaves, animals, and
property. Each household needed a legitimate male heir for its con-
tinuity and strength. Therefore, a father or his representative *kyrios*
would arrange the daughter's marriage for the purpose of "sowing
legitimate children." To ensure the legitimacy of heirs, girls were
married off right after puberty (13–15 years old), leaving their natal
home to join their husbands' *oikos*. Although we assume Antigone's
brother would have already arranged her marriage to her cousin and
Kreon's son, in the play, Kreon is her *kyrios*. He arranges her marriage
to death, and "Antigone sings for herself the very wedding hymn and
funeral dirge that Kreon has denied her."[20]

We do not tend to associate marriage with death, yet Greek
thought, literature, and ritual closely connects them. In the *Homeric
Hymn to Demeter*, an anonymous poem composed in the early seventh century BCE, Hades kidnaps Persephone to be his bride.[21] The
story of Hades and Persephone, frequently retold and referenced,
became a motif of marrying death. The connection in daily life was

[20] Rehm (1994) 64.
[21] Rayor (2004) 17.

also clear. Girls married in their young teens to men who were usually twice their age and had a high mortality rate in childbirth.[22] Infant mortality was high as well. A funeral could indeed follow swiftly after a wedding, transforming "the melody / of weddings to the sound of wailing dirges."[23] In addition, wedding and funeral rites, in which women played a crucial role, had many similarities. The bride and corpse were washed, dressed, anointed, and either veiled (bride) or shrouded (corpse). Both journeyed to a new home, led by a procession of family and friends carrying torches, with song and dance, blessings, gifts, and a feast.[24] *Antigone* makes those connections explicit in marrying Antigone to death in her last scene instead of to Kreon's son, her betrothed.

Language

Kreon and Antigone do not speak the same language, or rather they use the same words to mean very different things, with disastrous consequences. The Greek word *nomos* (the root of "economy," *oikos-nomos*) means custom and law. Although it was the traditional custom for family to bury their dead, Kreon's law forbids Polynices' burial. Antigone and Kreon both act according to their own understanding of *nomos*.

The word *philos* can refer to "kin" (family bound by kinship) or simply to a friend bound by ties of affection. These categories are particularly important in the traditional heroic ethic, which valorizes helping friends (*philoi*) and harming enemies.[25] Kreon uses one

---

[22] Demand (1994) 102: "women who give birth before the age of seventeen have a higher mortality rate than older women."

[23] Rayor (1991) 124: Erinna.

[24] Rehm (1994) 29.

[25] Blundell (1989).

meaning of *philos*, "friend," whereas Antigone uses the other, "close relative or loved one." Polynices attacked Thebes and so was no friend of the state; to Kreon, Polynices was not *philos*. Even so, Polynices was still Antigone's brother; to Antigone, Polynices remained irrevocably *philos*.

TRANSLATION

This introduction provides a background to the play, whereas the notes provide more detailed explanations of words, lines, and connections more apparent in the Greek. All the supplementary material is based on what students, teachers, directors, and casts needed or wanted to know. The bibliography lists a very small selection of the extensive fine resources available on ancient Greek drama and performance, and specifically on Antigone.

My goal for this *Antigone* was to produce an accurate translation that reads well and works well as a script for performance. I aimed for precision in meaning, and where I could not make it both precise and playable, I put an explanation in the notes. The experience of reading a translation of drama should be as close as possible to that of reading and hearing the Greek text. Rather than close down possibilities, it is the translator's responsibility to keep options of interpretation as open and rich as those available to readers of the original Greek. For performance, the language must be clear and work in speech. Can the actors say these lines and the audience understand them – in a single hearing and at the tempo in which they should be spoken or sung?

My translation was tempered in the fire of two productions, two courses in advanced Greek, and four courses in translation (mythology, classical world, and ancient religion). A week-long translation workshop with poets on the island of Paros in Greece helped refine two choral odes. An outreach session on *Antigone* for local high school teachers led a year later to the second production and a few more adjustments. The translation process involved colleagues in classics and theater, students in a variety of courses, international poets, my family, and area teachers and audiences.

The premiere production of this translation was by far the most critical to its development. In winter 2009, GVSU theater director Karen Libman and I collaborated with twenty-one students enrolled in the Classical Theatre Workshop to study, rehearse, and stage *Antigone*. Working closely with director and actors, I fine-tuned the translation into an actable script. Some lines looked fine on paper, but did not sound right when spoken by actors. In Antigone's dirge, the words "Mt. Sipylos" sounded like "syphilis," completely destroying the mood![26] Hearing lines aloud and in action triggered most of the revisions. Many times, students' questions or suggestions led to further revisions. If participants had questions, I either adjusted the translation or added information to the introduction or notes. The rehearsals resulted in more than one hundred changes – some involving a single word, others whole passages. The rhythms of speech and interaction shaped the translation.

I use the more common Latinized spelling of some names for the sake of familiarity (Oedipus) and pronunciation (Haemon); otherwise, I use the Greek forms (Kreon). For the Greek text, I primarily followed Mark Griffith's *Sophocles: Antigone* (Cambridge, 1999).

---

[26] This is the only place name left out of the translation.

Scene List

Opening Scene 1–99
Antigone
Ismene

Entrance Song of the Chorus 100–61

Scene Two 162–331
Kreon
Chorus
Guard

Second Song of the Chorus 332–75

Scene Three 376–581
Chorus Leader
Guard
Kreon
Antigone
Ismene

Third Song of the Chorus 582–625

Scene Four 626–780
Chorus Leader

Kreon

Haemon

Fourth Song of the Chorus 781–800

Scene Five 801–943

Chorus Leader

Antigone

Kreon

Fifth Song of the Chorus 944–87

Scene Six 988–1114

Tiresias

Kreon

Chorus Leader

Sixth Song of the Chorus 1115–54

Scene Seven 1155–1256

Messenger

Chorus

Eurydice

Scene Eight 1257–1353

Chorus Leader

Kreon

Messenger

Characters enter and exit through the doors into the palace (*skenê*) or on the wing side paths (*parodoi*). One path leads from the city (CP) and the other to the battlefield or burial grounds (BP). The chorus enters and exits on the *parodoi*.

Cast of Characters

ANTIGONE	*Daughter of Oedipus and Jocasta*
ISMENE	*Antigone's sister*
CHORUS	*Theban elders*
KREON	*Jocasta's brother, Antigone's uncle*
GUARD	
HAEMON	*Kreon's son*
TIRESIAS	*Seer*
MESSENGER	
EURYDICE	*Kreon's wife*

SILENT ATTENDANTS OF KREON, TIRESIAS, AND EURYDICE

Antigone

by Sophocles

SCENE 1:

Antigone enters from city path (CP); Ismene enters from
skenê.

ANTIGONE
My dear heart, Ismene, more than blood-sister,
is there even one thing from the evils of Oedipus
that Zeus doesn't inflict on the two of us still living?
There is no pain or disaster,
shame or dishonor that I have not seen   5
among these evils of yours and mine.
Now what is the new proclamation they say
the commander has just made to the whole city?
Did you hear anything? Or didn't you notice
that evils from our enemies advance upon our kin?   10

ISMENE
No word of our family, sweet or painful,
has come to me, Antigone,
not since the two of us lost our two brothers,
dead in one day by each other's hands.
Since the Argive army left this very night,   15
I know nothing more,
whether my fortune is brighter or doomed.

ANTIGONE
I thought so. I took you outside
the courtyard gate so you alone could hear.

ISMENE
What is it? You look like you're brooding over some news.   20

ANTIGONE
Well, hasn't Kreon honored one of our brothers
with proper rites, while refusing the other burial?
They say he buried Eteokles
with true observance of justice and custom,
honored below among the dead.   25
But the wretched corpse of Polynices?
They say, by proclamation to the citizens,
that no one may bury him or cry aloud,
that he be left unmourned, unburied, a sweet treasure
for birds spying him to eat at their pleasure.   30
That's what they say our good Kreon has proclaimed
to you and me – yes, to me, too.
He comes here to proclaim once more
to any who haven't heard. He's not treating this
as some minor matter – whoever would take action   35
is sentenced to death by public stoning in the city.
There you have it. You will soon reveal
whether you run true to your noble birth or not.

ISMENE
Poor sister, if that's how things stand,
what more could I offer to do or undo?   40

ANTIGONE
Consider whether you will share the burden and work together.

ISMENE
With what risk? What are you thinking of?

ANTIGONE
Will your hand join mine to lift his body?

ISMENE
What? Do you intend to bury him, forbidden in Thebes?

ANTIGONE
He's my brother and – like it or not – yours, too.   45
I will not be caught betraying him.

ISMENE
Stubborn! Even though Kreon has spoken against it?

ANTIGONE
He has no right to keep me from my own.

ISMENE
Oimoi! Think, my sister, how our father,
hateful, infamous, was destroyed   50
by discovering his own crimes,
striking his eyes with his own blinding hands.
Second, mother and wife, both in one,
ended her life with a twisted noose.
Third, two brothers in one day   55
killed their miserable selves, completing
a shared doom in each other's hands.
Now, consider again that the two of us left
will be utterly destroyed if in violence against the law
we transgress the decree and power of the king.   60
We need to recognize that we are women,
not meant to fight against men.
Since we are ruled by those more powerful,
we must obey now and in yet more painful ways.
I beg those below the earth   65
for pardon since I'm forced in this matter.

I will obey the authorities.
To do something so extreme makes no sense.

ANTIGONE
I won't insist, nor if you change your mind,
would your assistance please me.   70
Do as you think fit. I will bury him,
and doing so, will find a noble death.
Having dared a holy crime, I will lie with
the one I loved, and be loved. I must satisfy
those below far longer than those here   75
since I'll lie there forever. But if you think it's right,
keep dishonoring what the gods honor.

ISMENE
I do no dishonor, but it goes against my nature
to act in violence against the people.

ANTIGONE
You can make these excuses. I will go   80
to heap up a burial mound for my dearest brother.

ISMENE
Oimoi, Antigone, I'm afraid for you!

ANTIGONE
Don't worry about me. Set your own fate right.

ISMENE
At least don't tell anyone else what you're doing.
Hide the secret and I will too.   85

ANTIGONE
Oimoi, call it out! Your silence will earn you
far more hatred than if you proclaim it aloud.

ISMENE
You have a hot heart for cold matters.

ANTIGONE
I know I satisfy the ones I truly must please.

ISMENE
If you can. But you desire the impossible. 90

ANTIGONE
Then as soon as I lose strength, I'll stop.

ISMENE
It's not fitting to hunt the impossible in the first place.

ANTIGONE
Keep talking and I'll hate you, and you'll justly
lie beside your dead brother as an enemy.
But let me, and my ill-conceived plan, 95
suffer this dreadful fate – Nothing I will suffer
could be so terrible as to keep me from a noble death.

ISMENE
Go if you think it's right. Even though you act
without sense, to your family you are truly dear.

Antigone exits burial path (BP); Ismene exits skenê.
Entrance Song: Chorus enters CP.

CHORUS
Ray of sun, the loveliest 100
light ever to appear
in seven-gated Thebes,
you have come at last,

eye of golden day, shining
above the streams of Dirce.   105
The Argive with his white shield,
who fled in full armor,
you goaded by a sharper bit
into headlong flight,

who Polynices raised against our land   110
in his contentious quarrel.
That man, a screaming eagle
soaring over the land
with wings of white snow,
one among the many armed warriors   115
in crested helmets of horse-hair.

Hovering above our roofs,
poised to swallow the seven gates
surrounded by bloodthirsty spears,
before his jaws were sated   120
on our blood, he left
before the pine torch of Hephaistos
consumed our crown of towers.
Clamor of Ares
all around – matched in battle,   125
conquest by the Theban serpent.

Since Zeus despises
boasts of an arrogant tongue,
seeing them swarm against us
with presumptuous flash of gold,   130
he struck with his thunderbolt
the one on the high ramparts

right as he began his victory cry.

He plunged to the solid earth
ablaze, who until then raged   135
with Bacchic madness, and exhaled
blasts of most hostile gales.
Things did not turn out
as he had planned,
and to the rest, powerful Ares,   140
striking hard, dealt other fates:

the seven captains at the seven gates,
face to face with seven equals, left
their bronze shields, fee to Zeus the Battle-turner.
All except the hating two, sprung   145
from the same father and mother, who planted
their double-edged spears through each other,
together sharing a common death.

Now great-named Victory
has come rejoicing with   150
Thebes of the many chariots.
Let us forget the war. Let us
go round to all the temples of the gods,
and dance all night and sing,
and may Theban Dionysos,   155
Earthshaker, lead the way!

CHORUS LEADER
Now here comes the king of the land,
Kreon son of Menoeceus, new ruler

through recent fortunes from the gods.
What plan is he piloting that he summoned   160
by proclamation this special council of elders?

SCENE 2:

Kreon enters skenê.

KREON
Men, the affairs of state, wildly shaken
by the gods, have steadied aright again.
You, out of all the rest, I summoned here,
knowing well that you always   165
honored the power of the throne of Laius.
And again, when Oedipus set aright the state
and after he perished, you still stood
beside his sons with sound counsel.
Yet, since they were destroyed   170
by a double destiny in a single day, striking
and struck with their own stained hands,
I now hold all the power and the throne
by being next of kin to those destroyed.
It is impossible to learn the spirit,   175
mind, and judgment of any man
until he is tested in office and laws.
Whoever does not pursue the best policies
to steer the entire state,
but locks tight his tongue out of some fear,   180
has always seemed to me the worst.
And whoever thinks a friend more important

than his fatherland, I say he is nothing.
Let all-seeing Zeus be my witness:
I would not wait silently, watching ruin   185
rather than deliverance advance on the city.
I could never consider any man my friend
who is an enemy of the state, knowing that
this ship keeps us safe and only by sailing
it straight can we determine our friends.   190
I will strengthen this state with such laws.
Therefore, I have proclaimed to the people
related laws concerning the sons of Oedipus.
Eteokles, who died fighting for this city,
who bested everyone with his spear,   195
we buried and performed all holy rites
offered to the noble dead below.
But Polynices, his own brother,
who returned from exile seeking to incinerate
his fatherland and the gods of his family,   200
who wished to consume kindred blood,
to lead Thebans into slavery –
it has been proclaimed throughout the city
that no one honor him with burial or mourning,
but leave him unburied, a corpse devoured   205
by birds and dogs, foul to see.
Such is my judgment. Never in my hands
will the evil surpass the just in honor.
But whoever thinks well of the state
will be honored by me dead or alive.   210

CHORUS
You can do these things, son of Menoeceus,

to the one hostile to the city and the one well-disposed.
You have the power, I suppose, to enact any law
concerning the dead and those of us who live.

KREON
Now you must watch over my edicts.   215

CHORUS
Impose this task on someone younger.

KREON
No, guards already watch the corpse.

CHORUS
What else would you command?

KREON
Not to collaborate with those who may disobey.

CHORUS
No one is such a fool as to love death.   220

KREON
And that is the punishment.
But greed often ruins men.

Guard enters BP.

GUARD
My lord, I can't say I'm breathless
from speeding here on light feet.
My thoughts kept stopping me on the path,   225
wheeling me around to turn back.
My heart had a dialogue saying:
"Stupid, why go where you will be punished?"
"Crazy, you dare delay again? If Kreon hears it
from another man, how will you not pay?"   230

My mind in turmoil, reluctance slowed the way
and thus a short journey became long.
At last, however, coming here to you won out.
And if I would say nothing, I will speak nevertheless.
I come clutching the hope   235
that I might suffer nothing beyond my fate.

KREON
What caused all this anxiety?

GUARD
First, I want to tell you about myself.
I didn't do the deed or see whoever did.
In fairness, why should I fall into trouble?   240

KREON
You aim well yet fence around the affair.
Clearly, eventually, you will reveal something strange.

GUARD
Terrible events, as you know, call for much caution.

KREON
Won't you ever tell the tale and then remove yourself?

GUARD
I'll tell you: someone just now buried the corpse   245
and left after sprinkling thirsty dust on its skin
and performing the sacred rites as required.

KREON
What did you say? What man would dare?

GUARD
I don't know. No stroke of pick or hoe

had disturbed the dirt. The earth was hard   250
and dry, unbroken, unmarked by wheel tracks.
Whoever did it left no sign.
When the morning sentry showed us,
a terrible amazement overcame us all.
Polynices was hidden, not by a mound,   255
but with a light dust, enough to avoid pollution.
No sign revealed the arrival of any beast
or dogs or tearing of his flesh.
Curses flew loudly among us,
guard accusing guard. It would have come   260
to blows in the end, with no one to prevent it.
To each one, someone else was the culprit,
no one was obvious, and everyone denied all knowledge.
We were ready even to lift red-hot iron in our hands,
pass through fire and swear oaths to the gods   265
not to have done it or to have any knowledge
of the planning or of the deed itself.
At last, when nothing more was gained by searching,
someone spoke who impelled everyone to bow
his head in fear, not able to contradict him   270
or to see how to avoid trouble if we agreed.
The suggestion was that the deed
must be reported to you and not covered up.
This won out and the lot condemns
ill-fated me to undertake this great job.   275
I come unwillingly before the unwilling, no doubt.
No one loves the messenger of bad news.

Chorus
King, the thought keeps occurring to me
whether this, perhaps, is an act of god.

KREON
Stop before your speech fills me with rage 280
and you be found foolish, despite your age.
What you said is intolerable,
that gods care about this corpse.
Would they honor him for his good deed,
burying the man who came to burn down 285
the columns of their temples and sacred offerings,
to scatter their land and their laws?
Do you see the gods honoring the wicked?
Impossible! But from the very start, men in the city
could scarcely bear these edicts and clamored against me, 290
shaking their heads in secret. They refused to bow their necks,
as they should, under the yoke of submission to me.
I know very well that those men led the guards
astray with bribes to commit this crime.
Nothing has become such an evil currency 295
among humans as silver. It ravages cities,
banishes men from their homes,
teaches and converts honest souls
to attend to shameful deeds.
It shows men how to practice villainies 300
and to know impiety of every kind.
But those hired hands accomplished the task
and so in time will pay the penalty.
As Zeus ever keeps my reverence,
hear this oath I swear to you: 305
If you don't find the culprit in this burial
and reveal him before my eyes,
Hades alone won't suffice for you,
until strung up alive you expose this arrogance,
so that hereafter you may know where profit 310

should come from, and learn that you
must not love profiting from every source.
From shameful gain
more men lie ruined than saved.

GUARD
Will you allow me to speak? Or shall I turn and go?   315

KREON
Don't you know that your words irritate me?

GUARD
Do they sting your ears or your mind?

KREON
Why would you gauge the location of my pain?

GUARD
The culprit annoys your mind; I your ears.

KREON
Oimoi! You are clearly born a babbler!   320

GUARD
And yet I never did that deed.

KREON
You did, betraying your life for silver.

GUARD
Puh! How terrible for the judge to misjudge!

KREON
All right, go ahead, play with "judgment."
But you'll see how shady gain causes pain   325

if you don't show me the culprit.

Kreon exits skenê.

GUARD
May he truly be found! Whether he is caught
or not, since luck decides that,
no way will you see me coming back.
For now, beyond my hope and reason,   330
I'm saved and owe the gods much thanks.

Guard exits BP.
Second Song

CHORUS
Of the many strange wonders,
none is more wondrous than man.
He sails across the gray sea
through stormy south winds,   335
engulfed by the waves.
He tills Gaia
year after year,
plowing with mules,
wearing down   340
eternal, inexhaustible Earth,
the oldest of gods.

He traps the flighty
race of birds,
tribes of wild beasts,   345
and creatures from the salty sea,
casting with a coiled net.

Cunning man. He masters
with inventions the wild
animals roaming the hills,   350
tames the shaggy horse
and the untiring mountain bull,
leading them under the yoke.

Language and thought quick as wind
and the temper for city laws   355
he taught himself, and how to escape
exposure to hard frost
and arrows of heavy rain –
ingenious. He confronts no event
without his ingenuity.   360
From Hades alone
will he make no escape,
though devising refuge
from incurable disease.

With skillful technology,   365
clever beyond imagination,
sometimes he inches towards evil,
other times to good.
Who honors the laws of the land
and the oath-bound justice of the gods   370
is high in his city. But he has no city
if he joins the wicked in daring.
May he not share my hearth
nor share my thoughts,
whoever acts that way.   375

Scene 3:

Guard enters BP with Antigone.

Chorus Leader
What divine apparition has appeared
here? How? Knowing this is the child
Antigone – how can I claim it is not?
O misery of a miserable father,
of Oedipus, what now?   380
No! Did they bring you here,
disloyal to the royal laws
and caught in some foolish act?

Guard
This is the one who did the deed;
we caught her burying him. Where is Kreon?   385

Chorus
Here he comes from the house, just in time.

Kreon enters skenê.

Kreon
What's going on? Is there good news?

Guard
My Lord, for mortals nothing is sworn impossible.
Second thoughts make a lie of intent.
I insisted I'd never come here again   390
because of your threats hailing down on me.
But, since joy beyond the boundary of hope
extends like no other pleasure,
I came, although I swore it impossible on my oath,

to bring this girl, who was captured adorning   395
the grave. The lot was not cast this time,
but this is my bit of Hermes' luck, no other's.
And now, my Lord, as you wish, take her,
judge her, convict her. But I am free,
justly released from these troubles.   400

KREON
You caught her where? How?

GUARD
She was burying that man. You know all of it.

KREON
Do you truly understand what you just said?

GUARD
Yes, I saw her bury the corpse against your orders.
Aren't my words plain and clear?   405

KREON
How was she seen and caught in the act?

GUARD
This was how it happened. When we came,
threatened by you with terrible things,
we swept away all the dust which covered
the corpse, and made the oozing body full naked.   410
We sat perched on a high hill upwind,
fled so the stench of it not strike us,
each man busy rousing the next with noisy
abuse, if anyone should be careless of this labor.
So we passed the time until the bright   415

orb of sun stood in mid heaven
and the heat burned. Suddenly, a whirlwind
raised up a dust storm, grief from heaven,
filling the plane, tormenting every leaf
on the trees, stuffing the vast air full.   420
Closing our eyes, we endured the divine plague.
And when it departed after a long while,
we saw this child. She wailed aloud in bitterness
like the sharp cry of a bird discovering
the bed orphaned of its nestlings.   425
So she, too, when she saw the corpse bare,
wailed in mourning and called out
evil curses on whoever had done it.
Straightaway she bore thirsty dust in her hands,
and lifting high the well-hammered bronze pitcher,   430
anointed the body with three pourings of libations.
When we saw, we immediately rushed forward,
all together hunting her down, she not a whit frightened.
We asked about her earlier actions and those now.
She stood firm, denying utterly nothing,   435
which was both sweet and painful to me.
To have fled from evils oneself
is most sweet, but to lead friends to evil
is painful. But everything is less important
to me than my own safety.   440

KREON
You there, hanging your head,
do you admit or deny that you did this?

ANTIGONE
I did it and I do not deny it.

KREON

Guard, go where you wish,
free of this heavy charge.   445

Guard exits BP.

But you, tell me and make it brief:
Did you know that the burial was forbidden by proclamation?

ANTIGONE

I knew. How could I not? It was clear.

KREON

And yet you dared overstep these laws?

ANTIGONE

I did not hear Zeus proclaiming it.   450
Justice, who dwells with the gods below,
did not determine such laws for human beings.
I believed your mortal proclamation
had no such strength that you could override
the unwritten and unchanging rules of the gods.   455
Not just for now or yesterday, these rules live
always; no one knows when they first appeared.
I would not risk the punishment of the gods
for fear of the will of any man.
I knew very well that I would die, of course,   460
even if you had not proclaimed it. If I die
before my time, I call it pure gain.
Whoever lives among so many evils, as I do,
how can he not gain by dying?
So for me to meet this fate is no grief.   465
If I had dared to leave
my mother's dead son a corpse unburied,

for that I would grieve. But not for this.
If to you I seem to have done a foolish thing,
perhaps I'm charged with folly by a fool.   470

CHORUS
Clearly, a fierce daughter from a fierce father.
She doesn't understand how to back away from trouble.

KREON
Only know that minds too stubborn
fall hardest, and the strongest iron
heated extra-hard by fire is   475
shattered and crushed most surely.
I know that high-spirited horses
can be tamed with a small bit –
a slave is not allowed big thoughts.
She fully understood how to act arrogantly   480
when she transgressed the prescribed laws.
Doubly arrogant afterwards,
she exults in it and laughs.
Now I'm no man and she's the man,
if this unchecked power lies with her.   485
Whether she is my sister's daughter or closer
blood than my family at our shrine to Zeus,
she – and her sister – shall not escape
a most terrible fate. Yes, I charge Ismene
equally in planning this burial.   490
Summon her. I saw her inside just now,
raving, out of her mind.
The heart first reveals the criminal
as it contrives a crooked plan in the shadows.

And how I hate when someone caught   495
in the act wants to pretty it up.

ANTIGONE
You caught me – what more do you want than to kill me?

KREON
Nothing more. Then I have everything.

ANTIGONE
So why delay? Nothing you say
gives me pleasure. May it never!   500
And I please you just as little.
Yet how could I have won glory
more glorious than covering my own brother
in a grave? Everyone here would agree,
if fear didn't lock up their tongues.   505
But kingship is fortunate in many ways
and it can do and say what it wishes.

KREON
You alone of these Thebans see it that way.

ANTIGONE
They see it, too. But they shut their mouths for you.

KREON
Are you not ashamed to think so differently from them?   510

ANTIGONE
To honor those from the same womb is no shame.

KREON
Wasn't the one who died on the other side also blood kin?

ANTIGONE
Blood kin from one mother and the same father.

KREON
Then why offer tribute that dishonors Eteokles?

ANTIGONE
The lifeless corpse will not bear witness to this. 515

KREON
Yes, if you honor him and the irreverent just the same.

ANTIGONE
It was not some slave, but his brother who died.

KREON
Trying to sack this land, while the other defended it.

ANTIGONE
Even so, Hades desires these traditions.

KREON
But the good man shuns an equal portion with the bad. 520

ANTIGONE
Who knows if that is sacred below?

KREON
An enemy is never a friend, not even when dead.

ANTIGONE
My nature is not to join in hating, but in loving.

KREON
Go below now and love the dead, if you must love.
While I live, no woman shall rule me. 525

Ismene enters skenê.

CHORUS LEADER
Here comes Ismene by the gates,
raining sisterly tears.
A cloud over her brows
mars her flushed face,
drenching her fair cheeks.   530

KREON
You, lurking like a viper in my house,
secretly draining me – I did not know
I fed double ruin and revolutions against the throne.
Tell me, will you confess that you shared
in this burial, or will you swear you know nothing?   535

ISMENE
I did the deed, if she consents;
I join her and bear the blame.

ANTIGONE
But Justice will not allow you;
you weren't willing and I didn't share the deed.

ISMENE
In your sea of troubles, I'm not ashamed   540
to make myself a shipmate in your suffering.

ANTIGONE
Hades and those below witnessed whose deed it was.
I do not love kin who are kin only in words.

ISMENE
My sister, no! Don't deny me the honor

to die with you and to sanctify our dead. 545

ANTIGONE
Don't share my death nor claim for yourself
what you did not touch. It's enough that I die.

ISMENE
How can life be dear to me, abandoned by you?

ANTIGONE
Ask Kreon. He's the one you care about.

ISMENE
Why hurt me, when it doesn't help you? 550

ANTIGONE
If I mock, I mock you in grief.

ISMENE
Then how may I still help you, even now?

ANTIGONE
Save yourself. I don't begrudge you an escape.

ISMENE
Oimoi, miserable me! Am I to fail in your death, too?

ANTIGONE
You chose to live and I to die. 555

ISMENE
But not with my thoughts unspoken.

ANTIGONE
Your thoughts seemed right to one side, mine to the other.

ISMENE
Yet for both of us the fault is equal.

ANTIGONE
Be brave! You live, but my soul died
long ago, so that I might help the dead.   560

KREON
One of these girls, I tell you, has just now shown
that she's as crazy as the other has been from birth.

ISMENE
My king, not even innate sense
remains for those with bad fortune.

KREON
Yours left when you chose to do bad deeds with her.   565

ISMENE
What life is left for me alone, without her?

KREON
Do not speak of her; she no longer exists.

ISMENE
Will you kill the bride of your own son?

KREON
There are other fields to plow.

ISMENE
Not as good a fit for him as she.   570

KREON
I hate bad wives for sons.

ISMENE
Dearest Haemon, how your father dishonors you!

KREON
You and that marriage cause too much grief!

ISMENE
Will you really rob your son of her?

KREON
Hades will stop the marriage for me.   575

ISMENE
It is decided, it seems, that she dies.

KREON
Decided by both you and me. No more delays.
Escort them inside, servants. From now on,
they must be women and not freely roam.
Even the bold flee when they see Hades   580
looming over their life.

Two servants escort Antigone and Ismene, exit skenê.
Third Song

CHORUS
Blest are those whose lives have not tasted evils.
But for those whose house
has been shaken by a god,
no blight is lacking.   585
It imbues the generations,
as when a wave
swept by Thracian gales
runs over the darkness of the depths,

stirring black sand   590
up from the sea floor, striking
with a roar the wind-worn headlands.

I see the sorrows of the house of Labdacus
pile on the sorrows
of the dead from long ago,   595
each generation does not free the next;
no, a god casts them down
and gives no release.
Now the bloody dust of the gods below
again severs the light   600
which the last root had spread
in the house of Oedipus –
folly of speech and Fury of mind.

What man's transgression, Zeus,
could restrain your power?   605
Not all-subduing Sleep
nor the years' untiring months.
Ruler unaging in time,
you dwell in the marble
radiance of Olympos.   610
In the present, future
and past, this law
will endure: Nothing vast
enters human life without ruin.

Hope, who wanders wide,   615
benefits many men, but deceives
many with careless desires.

It misleads the one who knows nothing
until he has burned his foot in the fire.
As a wise man said   620
in the famous proverb,
evil can appear good
to one whose mind
a god leads to ruin.
Then he has so little time without ruin.   625

SCENE 4:

Haemon enters CP.

CHORUS LEADER
Here's Haemon, your youngest son.
Does he come to mourn
the doom of his betrothed bride,
Antigone, fiercely grieving
the cheating of his marriage-bed?   630

KREON
Soon we'll know more than the seers.
Son, after hearing the official decree for your intended bride,
you haven't come to rage against your father, have you?
Or are we dear to you no matter what we do?

HAEMON
Father, I am yours. You guide me straight when   635
you have the best judgment, and that I will follow.
To me, no marriage would be worth more
than your good direction.

KREON
Yes, son, you must hold that in your heart
and stand behind your father's judgment in every way.   640
For that reason, men pray to produce
attentive sons in their houses,
so that, like their fathers, they may pay back
an enemy with evil and honor a friend.
What else would you say about a man who plants   645
worthless children, but that he harvests
labors for himself and laughter for his enemies?
Now, son, never throw out your good sense
just for the pleasure of a woman,
knowing that it becomes a cold embrace,   650
an evil wife for a bedmate at home.
What could be a greater ulcer than an evil spouse?
Spit her out as an enemy –
let that girl go to Hades to marry someone.
I caught her in open defiance,   655
she alone of all the citizens.
I won't make myself a liar before the city.
I will kill her. Let her sing about her Zeus,
god of kindred blood. If I nurture disorder
in my own family, how much more so in others?   660
Whoever is dutiful in his own household,
will also appear just in the city.
And such a man, I'm confident,
would rule well or be willing to be ruled.
When posted in a storm of spears,   665
he'd remain a just and good comrade-in-arms.
But whoever oversteps and assaults the laws
or thinks to command his rulers,

may never win praise from me.
Whoever the state appoints must be obeyed 670
in little things, in justice and its opposite.
For there is no greater evil than anarchy.
Anarchy destroys states, overturns households.
It makes allied forces erupt in flight.
But when those forces succeed, 675
it's obedience that saves many lives.
Thus one must defend order,
and in no way be less than a woman.
Better felled by a man, if need be,
than called weaker than women. 680

CHORUS
If the passage of time hasn't deceived us,
you seem to speak sensibly.

HAEMON
Father, gods produce good sense in men,
which is the highest of all possessions.
I couldn't say – may I never be able! – 685
to say that you speak amiss.
Yet alternate paths may turn out well, too.
I'm in the habit of looking out for you
in everything anyone says or does or faults.
Your eye is terrifying for citizens 690
speaking words you don't delight in hearing.
But I can hear things under darkness,
how the city weeps for this girl,
of all women most undeserving to perish
most evilly for the most noble deeds. 695
Who, her brother fallen in bloody battle,

didn't leave him unburied to be destroyed
by flesh-eating dogs or some birds of prey.
Is she not worthy to win golden honor?
Such the dark rumor silently spreads.   700
I have no possession more valuable
than your good welfare.
What adornment is greater for children
than a father's thriving glory, or for a father than his son's?
Don't set one standard for yourself alone,   705
that whatever you say is correct and nothing else.
Whoever thinks that he alone contains good sense
in speech or spirit, which no other has,
when opened up is found to be a blank tablet.
No, even if a man is wise, there's no shame   710
in learning many things and not being too rigid.
By the winter-swollen streams you see
which trees bend and save even their twigs,
but the stiff are destroyed root and branch.
And when a man in power keeps taut   715
his ship's rigging and yields not a bit,
he overturns the ship and navigates upside down.
Relax your anger and let yourself change.
If any judgment can come from me, a younger man,
I say it is best by far for a man   720
to be naturally full of all knowledge.
But if not, as is nature's usual way,
when someone speaks wisely, it is good to learn.

Chorus
King, it's suitable for you, if he says something opportune,
to learn, and you, Haemon, from him, since both have spoken wisely. 725

KREON
Shall even men of such an age be taught
wisdom by a man of such an age?

HAEMON
About nothing unjust. If I am young, one must
not look at years more than facts.

KREON
Respecting rebels is a fact? 730

HAEMON
I would urge no one to respect the wicked.

KREON
But hasn't she been seized by just such a disease?

HAEMON
All the people of Thebes deny it.

KREON
Will the public tell me what I must command?

HAEMON
Don't you see that you're talking like an adolescent? 735

KREON
Must someone other than myself tell me how to rule this land?

HAEMON
The public is not the same as one man.

KREON
Is the state not considered the ruler's?

HAEMON
You would rule a desert well alone.

KREON
He, it seems, allies with the woman.   740

HAEMON
Only if *you* are the woman – my concern is for you.

KREON
By accusing your father, you scoundrel?

HAEMON
Yes, because I see you erring against justice.

KREON
I err in respecting my own authority?

HAEMON
You don't respect it, trampling on the gods' honors.   745

KREON
Foul creature, inferior to a woman.

HAEMON
At least you won't catch me subject to something shameful.

KREON
Yet all your words are for her.

HAEMON
And for you and me and the gods below.

KREON
She won't be alive for you to marry.   750

HAEMON
Then she will die and in dying destroy another.

KREON
What! Does your daring proceed to threats?

HAEMON
What threat to speak against empty judgments?

KREON
You'll regret lecturing me, as you're empty of sense yourself.

HAEMON
If you weren't my father, I would say that you lack good sense.   755

KREON
You woman's slave, don't cajole me.

HAEMON
Do you wish to speak, but never listen?

KREON
What! By Olympos, listen here: you will not
abuse me with reproaches and rejoice.
Bring that hated thing, so that right now, before his eyes   760
and in his presence, she can die beside her bridegroom.

HAEMON
No! Not in front of me, never think that!
She will not be killed beside me
and you will never set eyes on my face.
Rave on, live with whatever kin are still willing.   765

Haemon exits BP.

CHORUS
Your son, King, stormed out in anger.
A young heart grieves hard.

KREON

Let him go. Let him act more arrogant than a man should.
But he will not rescue these girls from their fate.

CHORUS

Do you really intend to kill both of them?   770

KREON

No, not the girl who didn't touch him. You speak wisely.

CHORUS

How do you plan to kill the other one? What is her fate?

KREON

Taking her to a deserted path away from people,
I will hide her alive in a rocky cavern,
setting out enough food to avoid a curse,   775
so that Thebes may escape all blame.
And there, praying to Hades, the only god
she reveres, perhaps she won't happen to die,
or at least she will learn that
it is a waste of labor to revere Hades.   780

Kreon sits on throne. Or possibly exits skenê.
Fourth Song

CHORUS

Eros, invincible in battle,
Passion, who ravishes wealth,
you stay the night
on the soft cheeks of a girl,
and roam the open sea   785
and through meadowland homes.
None of the immortal gods

and no ephemeral
human can escape you;
whoever has you is mad. 790

You warp the minds of the just
to do injustice for their own ruin;
you even stirred up
this bloody quarrel among kinsmen.
Radiant desire in the eyes 795
of the bride ready to bed prevails.
It shares authority
with the great laws,
since the goddess Aphrodite
plays there, unbeatable. 800

SCENE 5:

Antigone enters skenê.

CHORUS LEADER
Now I, too, am carried beyond laws
at this sight. I can no longer
hold back streams of tears
when I see Antigone nearing
the bridal chamber that gives rest to all. 805

ANTIGONE *(sings)*
Look at me, elders of my fatherland,
traversing the last road,
gazing upon the last
light of sun and never again.

But Hades, who grants rest to all,   810
leads me still alive
to the shores of Acheron.
No share of wedding hymns,
no wedding song sung
for me at my marriage.   815
Instead, I will wed Death.

CHORUS *(chant)*
Are you not gaining glory and praise
as you depart for the hidden place of the dead?
Neither struck with wasting disease
nor sharing in the wages of the sword,   820
but by your own law, you alone of mortals
will descend alive to Hades.

ANTIGONE *(sings)*
I have heard tell the saddest death
of a guest from Phrygia, Tantalos'
daughter, high on the mountain   825
where a growth of stone,
like clinging ivy, subdued her.
They say that
rain and snow never leave Niobe
as she wastes away,   830
and below ever-weeping lids
her rocky sides stream.
Just like her, a god puts me to rest.

CHORUS *(chant)*
No, she is immortal and born of a god,
while we are mortals and born to die.   835

Yet it is a great thing to hear, when you die,
that you shared a portion with the godlike
while alive and then after death.

ANTIGONE *(sings)*
You mock me! By our fathers' gods,
why do you insult me before I'm gone,   840
while I'm still clearly in sight?
O city and the city's
prosperous men,
O streams of Dirce and sacred plain
of Thebes of the many chariots,   845
at least I win you to witness
how I'm sent by such laws
to the rock-enclosed prison
of this strange tomb, unmourned by my family.
Miserable and with no home   850
among the living or the dead,
I'm not alive, nor have I died.

CHORUS *(sing)*
Pressing on to the limits of daring,
child, you crashed hard
against the high throne of Justice.   855
You are paying for trouble from your father.

ANTIGONE *(sings)*
You touch my most painful thoughts,
a lament plowed over and over
for my father and for the whole
destiny of us all   860
in the famous line of Labdacus.

O the blight of the maternal bed
and the incestuous coupling
of my father and his ill-fated mother,
from what parents was my miserable self born!   865
I am returning to them,
cursed and unwed, to share their home.
Brother, you met with
an ill-fated marriage,
and by your death,   870
you kill me while I'm still alive.

CHORUS *(sing)*
Showing reverence is pious, no doubt.
But power, to those in power,
is in no way to be trampled on.
Your self-generated temper destroyed you.   875

ANTIGONE *(sing)*
No laments, no family, no bridal song,
miserable, I am led
on this road without delay.
No longer may I in misery see
the sacred eye of the sun.   880
No one weeps for my destiny;
none of my kin grieves aloud.

Kreon steps forward.

KREON
Don't you know that no one would ever stop singing
and moaning before dying, if it gained them time?
Take her quickly! When you have enclosed her,   885
as I said, in the vaulted tomb, abandon her
alone, deserted, whether she wishes to die

or to live entombed in such a shelter.
For we are pure concerning this girl.
In any case, she'll be deprived of a home above. 890

ANTIGONE
O tomb, bridal chamber, deep,
eternal crypt where I walk toward
my own kin, most of whom have perished
and Persephone has welcomed among the dead.
Last of them, and the worst off by far, 895
I will descend before reaching my portion of life.
I deeply nurse the hope that when I arrive
I'll be dear to my father, dear to you, mother,
and dear to you, my darling brother.
When you all died, with my own hands I washed 900
and dressed you and over your graves
I poured libations. Now, Polynices, laying out
your body, this is what I earn.
Yet, to sensible people, I did well to honor you.
I would never, if I had been the mother of children 905
or if my husband were dead and rotting,
have chosen this labor in violence against the people.
According to what custom do I say this?
A husband dead, there would be another for me,
and a child from another man, if I lost one. 910
But since my mother and father lie hidden in Hades,
no new brother could ever be born.
While I deeply honored you according to such custom,
I seemed to Kreon to do wrong
and to dare terrible things, my darling brother. 915
Now he seizes my hand and takes me away.
With no marriage bed, no wedding song,

not destined to marry or nurture children,
but deserted by loved ones and ill-fated,
alive I enter the cave of the dead.   920
What divine law have I transgressed?
Why should I, ill-fated, still look to the gods?
What ally can I invoke?
When I acted piously I was called impious.
If, to the gods, this truly is good,   925
through suffering, I will know I erred.
But if these men err, may they suffer no more
evil than they do unjustly to me.

CHORUS
Still the same blasts of spirit
from the same winds possess her.   930

KREON
For all this, her guards
will soon regret their slowness.

ANTIGONE
Oimoi! Your word has drawn
very near my death.

KREON
I do not at all encourage taking heart   935
that these plans will not be executed.

ANTIGONE
O Theban land, city of my father
and ancestral gods,
I am led away and delay no longer.
Behold, leaders of Thebes,   940
the only woman left in the royal line,

see what I suffer from such men
because I acted with reverence.

Antigone exits BP.
Fifth Song

Chorus
Danaë, too, endured relinquishing
heaven's light for a chamber bound   945
in bronze. She was hidden away,
imprisoned in a tomb-like tower.
Yet, dear child, honored for her ancestry,
she was the depository for Zeus' shower of golden seed.
But Destiny, whatever it may be,   950
is a strange, awful power:
neither wealth nor Ares,
a tower nor dark ships
beaten by the sea, may escape.

The hot-headed Edonian king,   955
son of Dryas, was bound by Dionysos
for his mocking temper
and confined in a rocky prison.
There the awful, blooming strength
of his madness ebbed away.   960
That man finally recognized the god
he assaulted with mad, taunting tongue,
when he tried to stop the god-possessed
women and the Bacchic fire,
and enraged the pipe-playing Muses.   965

Near the waters of the Dark Islands
of the double sea, the coasts

of Bosporus and Thracian Salmydessos,
there the neighboring god Ares
witnessed the cursed wounds   970
blinding Phineus' two sons.
His savage second wife
blinded them, their eye
sockets crying for vengeance,
gouged by her bloody   975
hands and shuttlepoints.

Wasting away in misery,
the suffering pair wept in agony,
sons born of a badly wed mother.
She descended from an ancient line,   980
grandchild of Erechtheus,
daughter of Boreas.
She was raised in distant caves
with her father's storm-winds,
like a horse winging over steep crags,   985
child of gods. But even over her,
immortal Destiny prevailed, my child.

SCENE 6:

Tiresias enters CP with boy.

TIRESIAS
Theban elders, we have come on the same road,
two seeing from the eyes of one.
Blind men travel best with a guide.   990

KREON
What is new, old Tiresias?

TIRESIAS
I will teach you – be persuaded by the seer.

KREON
I never resisted your prophecy before.

TIRESIAS
Therefore you steered the state on a straight course.

KREON
I can testify to having experienced your aid.   995

TIRESIAS
Consider that you now walk again on the razor-edge of fortune.

KREON
What is it? How I shudder at your words.

TIRESIAS
You will know when you hear the omens of my art.
As I took my place on the ancient seat of augury,
where I have a sanctuary for every bird,   1000
I heard an unfamiliar cry of birds
screeching with evil and barbaric frenzy.
I knew they were tearing each other bloody
with their talons – the whirring of wings spoke clearly.
In fear, I attempted to burn sacrifices   1005
on the flaming altars. But the fire of Hephaistos
would not flare up from the offerings –
the thighs melted oozing juices on the embers,
smoking and sizzling, the gall bladders

burst high in the air, and the thigh pieces   1010
dripped bare of their covering fat.
Such failed prophecies from unreadable sacrifices,
I learned from this boy.
He is my guide, as I am for others.
Now, the state suffers this disease from your counsel: 1015
The altars and sacrificial hearths, one and all,
birds and dogs fill with meat
from the ill-fated fallen son of Oedipus.
And so the gods no longer accept sacrificial
prayers or burnt offerings from us,   1020
no bird shrieks forth clear signs
after gorging on the rich blood of a slain man.
Think about these things, child.
For all human beings, to err is common.
When a man has erred and fallen into evil,   1025
he will not remain foolish and unlucky,
if he seeks a remedy and is not inflexible.
Willfulness incurs a charge of stupidity.
Give in to the dead – don't prod a corpse.
What valor in killing the dead again?   1030
I give good advice with good will for you. Learning
is sweetest if the advice is spoken for your gain.

KREON
Old man, everyone shoots arrows at me
like archers at a target. I've suffered
your prophetic art; the tribe of seers   1035
traded and delivered me long ago.
Make a profit, if you wish, bartering
electrum from Sardis and Indian gold.

You will not hide that man in a grave,
not even if Zeus' eagles wish to seize his meat   1040
and bear it to Zeus' own throne.
Not even from fear of that pollution will I
allow anyone to bury that man. For I know
that no human has the power to defile gods.
But, old Tiresias, even very clever people   1045
fall shamefully, when they utter
shameful words well for the sake of gain.

TIRESIAS
Puh! Does anyone know, do any consider that –

KREON
What? What commonplace do you speak?

TIRESIAS
– that the most powerful possession is good counsel?   1050

KREON
Just as, I believe, lack of judgment causes the most harm.

TIRESIAS
Yet you always were full of that disease.

KREON
I don't wish to speak foully against a prophet.

TIRESIAS
And yet you do, saying I foretell falsely.

KREON
Since prophets all love silver.   1055

TIRESIAS
And tyrants love shameful profit.

KREON
Do you understand you are talking about your commander?

TIRESIAS
I understand, since you saved this city through me.

KREON
You are a skilled prophet, but you love to do wrong.

TIRESIAS
You will incite me into declaring things unrevealed in my mind.   1060

KREON
Reveal them, only don't speak for profit.

TIRESIAS
Have I seemed that way to you so far?

KREON
Know you cannot barter my will.

TIRESIAS
Listen carefully now: you will not
complete many racing courses of the sun   1065
before you will give up one corpse
from your own loins in exchange for corpses,
because you have cast below one who belongs above,
making a living soul dishonorably dwell in a tomb,
while you keep here a corpse belonging to the gods below,   1070
without due portion, without burial rites, without holiness.
You have no right to the dead, nor do the gods
above, yet you violate them even now.
Hence, the Furies, the destructive avengers
of Hades and the gods, lie in ambush for you,   1075

so that you may be caught in the very same evils.
Consider whether my speech is covered in silver.
For a brief passage of time will reveal
the wailing of men and women in your house.
All the enemy states will be in great uproar   1080
whose mangled corpses were given burial rights
by dogs or wild beasts, or some winged bird,
carrying an unholy stench to the city hearths.
Since you taunt me, I have shot like an archer
such sure arrows in anger to the heart   1085
that you cannot outrun their heat!
Boy, lead us home.
He can shoot his temper at younger men
and learn to nurture a calmer tongue
and better attitude than he has now.   1090

Tiresias and Boy exit CP.

CHORUS
King, that man left with terrible prophecies.
We know truly that from the time
we have worn white hair instead of black,
he has never once spoken falsely to the state.

KREON
Yes, I know and my mind is in turmoil.   1095
To give in is terrible, but to ruin my soul
by resisting is also terrible.

CHORUS
One must take good counsel, child of Menoeceus.

KREON
What must I do? Tell me, I will obey.

CHORUS
Take the girl up from her rocky cave,   1100
and make a grave for the one lying dead.

KREON
This is your counsel? That it seems best to give in?

CHORUS
As quickly as possible, Lord, for swift-footed
harm from the gods cuts short fools.

KREON
Oimoi! It's hard, but I withdraw from doing what my heart   1105
resolves. One must not fight vainly with necessity.

CHORUS
Do this now! Go, do not leave it to others.

KREON
I shall go just as I am. Quick, servants,
go one and all, with axes in hand –
hurry to that place within sight.   1110
I myself, as my opinion has been reversed,
since I bound her, I personally will release her.
I fear that it is best to complete one's life
preserving the established customs.

Kreon exits BP.
Sixth Song

CHORUS
God of many names,   1115
Semele's glory,
son of loud-thundering Zeus,

tending famed Italy,
ruling Eleusis, open to all,
in Demeter's lap; Bacchus,   1120
you dwell in the bacchants'
mother city Thebes
by the flowing Ismenos
and land sown
with the savage dragon's teeth.   1125

The flare of smoky torches
and the Kastalian stream have seen you
above the twin peaks
where Korycian Nymphs
step in Bacchic dance.   1130
Ivy slopes of Mt. Nysa
and the shores green
with grapevines escort you,
while divine chants
cry out "Euoi!" to you   1135
who watch over Theban streets.

You honor Thebes
above all cities,
you and your lightning-
struck mother.   1140
Now, as violent sickness
grips the whole city,
come again with purifying step
over Mt. Parnassos
or by the moaning strait.   1145

O chorus leader of
the fire-breathing stars,
watcher of night voices,
son born from Zeus,
O lord, appear before us   1150
with your attending Thyiads,
who dance all night
in frenzy for you,
generous Dionysos!

SCENE 7:

Messenger enters BP.

MESSENGER
Neighbors of the house of Kadmos and Amphion,   1155
I could never praise or blame
a single human life as if it were settled,
for luck raises up and luck suddenly fells
both the lucky and the unlucky.
No one can predict the present.   1160
Kreon was to be envied, it seemed to me,
when he saved this Theban land from its enemies,
took on the country's monarchic rule,
and steered it straight, thriving with noble children.
And now all has been lost. For whenever a man's   1165
pleasure deserts him, I don't consider him
alive, but a living corpse.
Fill the house with great wealth, if you wish,
and live like a tyrant. But without joy,
I wouldn't pay a shadow of smoke   1170

for that life without pleasure.

CHORUS
What is your painful news about the king?

MESSENGER
They are dead, and the living are guilty of their death.

CHORUS
Who is the murderer? Who lies dead? Speak!

MESSENGER
Haemon has perished, bloodied by a royal hand. 1175

CHORUS
His father's or his own hand?

MESSENGER
His own, in anger at his father for murder.

CHORUS
Prophet, your words were proven right, after all.

MESSENGER
That being so, it is time to take counsel.

CHORUS
I see unhappy Eurydice, Kreon's wife, 1180
coming out of the house by chance,
or perhaps because she heard about her son.

Eurydice enters skenê.

EURYDICE
Men from town, I heard your words
as I was heading outside to invoke
Pallas Athena in prayer. 1185

I was unfastening the bolts of the gate,
when the utterance of evil upon my house
struck my ears. I fell back in fear
near my maidservants and fainted.
But whatever the tale was, tell it again.   1190
For, not untested in evil events, I will listen.

MESSENGER
Since I was there, dear mistress, I will speak
and not omit a word of the truth.
Why should I try to soothe you, when later
I would be exposed a liar? Truth is an ever-straight course.   1195
I was attending your husband as a guide
on the highest part of the plain, where Polynices'
unpitied, dog-mangled body still lay.
After praying to the Crossroad Goddess
and Plouton to gentle their tempers,   1200
we gave him the ritual bath, gathered and burned
what was left of him on newly cut branches,
and heaped up a high tomb of his native earth.
Then we walked toward the girl's rock-paved
bridal chamber, the cave of Hades.   1205
From afar, someone heard the shrill wailings
of a voice near the unhallowed entry
and reported to master Kreon.
As he crept nearer, an incoherent cry of misery
surrounded him. Groaning in anguish,   1210
he cried out: "O misery, am I a prophet?
Shall I crawl on the most unfortunate
path of all roads traveled?
The voice of my son greets me. Servants,

hurry! Standing near the tomb, look 1215
closely and enter the cave where stones
have been torn out, to its mouth. Do I hear
Haemon's voice or I am deluded by the gods?"
As our dispirited master commanded,
we did look closely. Far back in the tomb, 1220
we saw Antigone hanging by her neck,
suspended by a woven noose of linen.
Embracing her waist, he pressed against her,
bemoaning the destruction of his marriage bed
lost below, his father's deeds, and his unhappy bride. 1225
Kreon, seeing him, groaned in despair
and started toward him, wailing loudly:
"O reckless one, what have you done? What
were you thinking? What misfortune deranged you?
Come out, child, I beg you!" 1230
With wild eyes, his son stared at him,
spitting in his face and answering nothing.
He drew his double-edged sword,
but as his father rushed out in flight, he missed.
Ill-fated, angry at himself, he suddenly tensed 1235
and thrust the sword deep into his own side. Barely
conscious, he embraced the girl in his limp arms.
Panting, he spurted a quick stream
of bloody drops upon her white cheek.
He lies corpse upon corpse, receiving 1240
marriage rites at last, poor man, in Hades' house,
revealing to humankind how ill counsel
is by far the greatest evil for man.

Eurydice exits or begins to exit skenê.

CHORUS
What do you make of that? His wife gone
again, without saying a word good or bad. 1245

MESSENGER
I am amazed, but I'm nourished by hope
that the news of her child's suffering won't lead
to public mourning, but under her own roof, inside
with her servants, she'll begin lamenting the family's sorrow.
She is not untested in judgment and so not likely to err. 1250

CHORUS
I don't know. To me, too much silence
seems as ominous as loud weeping and wailing.

Eurydice's exit is complete.

MESSENGER
We will know whether she hides something
quietly held back in her raging heart
once I enter the house. You are right – 1255
too much silence is ominous.

Messenger exits skenê.

SCENE 8:

Kreon enters BP.

CHORUS LEADER
Here comes the king himself,
holding a clear memorial,
if it is right to say, to the ruins

of his own mistake, no other's.   1260

KREON *(sings)*
Oh! Deadly stubbornness,
the mistake of a foolish mind!
Behold the kindred
killers and the kindred dead
from my unlucky decisions. *Oimoi!*   1265
Oh! Child, so new to life, new to death,
oh woe, you died,
not sent from life by your doing,
but by my bad counsel.

CHORUS
Oimoi, you seem to see justice too late.   1270

KREON *(sings)*
Oimoi! I've learned,
miserable me. Some god struck
my head, then with full weight,
hurled me on savage paths,
trampling, toppling joy. *Oimoi!*   1275
Damn the pains of mortals, harsh pains.

Messenger enters skenê.

MESSENGER
Master, you seem to come bearing evils,
and have more in store,
those in your hands and those in the house
you will soon see.   1280

KREON
What evil could be even worse than these evils?

MESSENGER
Your wife, true mother of this corpse, is dead,
unhappy man, just now by freshly inflicted blows.

KREON *(sings)*
Oh! The haven of Hades hard to cleanse,
why me, why do you destroy me?   1285
What tale do you tell, you who bring
the sorrow of evil tidings to me?
Woe! You destroyed a ruined man anew.
What are you saying . . . telling me . . .
what new slaughter . . .   1290
heaped on his death – *oh!* –
my wife's corpse?

CHORUS
We can see, as she's no longer inside the house.

KREON *(sings)*
Oimoi!
I see this second evil, oh misery.   1295
What fate, what still awaits me?
Just now I hold in my hands my child,
yet now I see my wife facing me dead,
ah, poor mother,
oh, my poor child.   1300

MESSENGER
Over a keen-edged sword at the altar,
she released her eyes to darkness, after mourning
her marriage, empty first of dead Megareus
and now of Haemon, finally she cursed

your evil actions as child murderer. 1305

KREON *(sings)*
Oimoi!
I tremble with dread.
Why did no one strike me
in the chest with a double-edged sword?
I'm miserable, 1310
dissolved in misery.

MESSENGER
Before she died, she denounced you
as responsible for the doom of both sons.

KREON
How could she destroy herself in cold blood?

MESSENGER
By striking under her liver with her own hand 1315
when she heard of her son's keen suffering.

KREON *(sings)*
Oimoi! My responsibility for this
will never belong to another mortal.
I myself killed you –
O unhappy me, 1320
I speak the truth.
Oh come, servants,
take me quickly,
take me away.
I'm less than nothing. 1325

CHORUS
Your advice is profitable, if there's any profit

among evils. For briefest is best with evils about.

KREON *(sings)*
Hurry!
Let the loveliest doom
appear for me now,   1330
bringing my last day,
by far the best. Let it come,
when I no longer see another day.

CHORUS
In time. Other powers take care of such things.
Now you must care for what lies before you.   1335

KREON
But my prayer spoke my desire.

CHORUS
Then don't pray now. Deliverance
from destined calamity is impossible for mortals.

KREON *(sings)*
Take a worthless man away.
My child, I didn't mean to kill you,   1340
nor you, my wife.
Oimoi, misery!
I don't know
which to look at,
what to lean on.   1345
All in my hands is askew; in all else,
unbearable fate has crashed on my head.

Kreon exits skenê.

CHORUS *(chant)*
By far, good sense is the first principle
of happiness. One must not disrespect
what belongs to the gods.
Great blows punish
great boasting by arrogant men,
and teach good sense in old age.

Exodos

Note from a Stage Director

How do you produce a piece of classical theatre in a way that is relevant and provocative for a modern audience? I confronted this question while directing the inaugural production of Diane Rayor's newly translated *Antigone*, and the answers we (my cast of university actors and I) came up with resulted in a satisfying and engaging piece of theater for audience and cast members alike. The two concerns that seemed most relevant to our work as a university theater program were (1) making a story, well-known to its original Greek viewers, just as easy to understand for its twenty-first-century audience and (2) engaging the audience with the classical theatrical conventions of the Messenger and Chorus in innovative ways.

Antigone begins after Oedipus' death and the war in which Antigone's brothers kill each other. The Greek audience of 440s BCE would have known the family relationships and basic events surrounding the Theban cycle as well as many of my students know the story of Jesus. You can put dramaturgical notes in the program to help a modern audience get up to speed, but many audience members will not have the time or interest to read the notes before they

see the play. Nor did we want to add a prologue, as we had seen in
other productions. Instead, we addressed this issue of lack of familiarity by incorporating a family tree as the backdrop flat of our play.
There, right in front of the audience was a visual representation of
the House of Thebes – who begat whom, who was king when, etc. –
and it immediately helped establish relationships for an audience
with little or no foreknowledge of the story.

We also used costuming to help clarify class and rank. We had
no desire to do the play in period dress, traditional Greek robes
being rather cold for an outdoor production in April in Michigan!
Instead we wanted instant recognition. If a character wore a crown,
you assumed he was royal. Antigone and Ismene were the age of
schoolgirls; therefore, they should be dressed as such. Haemon fought
in the battle – therefore, he wore a uniform. We also wanted to achieve
some sort of immediate relevancy for the production, and although
period costuming adds majesty and accuracy, we were not abiding
by the conventions of the original period (such as only using three
actors with masks) so accuracy was not our goal: Significance was.
Majesty we could gain in other ways. Therefore, we used modern
costumes with archetype accents, a simple costume device to cue the
audience as to the status of the characters.

Scholars have commented that the Messenger's long exposition
is difficult for a contemporary viewer to follow. Yet the information
the Messenger brings in *Antigone* is pivotal to the plot. It is essential
that no one misses it! Our solution was to divide the Messenger
into two characters: Two Messengers tag-teamed the delivery of the
message. By having two Messengers, we changed the dynamic. The
Messengers spoke not only to the Chorus and Eurydice but also to
each other. Taking and breaking the message into two distinct voices
enlivened the scene both vocally and pictorially. We further involved
the Messengers in the discovery of Eurydice's body and even had
them help clear the stage after the king's lament.

But what of the Chorus? What of the long odes, which refer to many things that modern audiences do not know and were originally sung and danced? Scholarship on modern productions argues that the Chorus is frequently the most problematic part of a production, but that keeping the spectacle it provided is key to its success. We decided that the Chorus *should* sing and dance its long numbers. Therefore, I composed original music with a Greek flavor and choreographed dances for every long choral passage. We were fortunate to have musicians in the Chorus who played reed instruments that, although not the same as those in Sophocles' time, were at least in the same family of instrumentation. The spectacle of song and dance added majesty and also evoked ancient practices with a modern flair.

We also strove to homogenize the Chorus. The elders of Thebes wore neutral black pants, long-sleeved shirts, and half-masks to cover individual actor features. The Chorus remained onstage and frequently became a part of the background spectacle. The idea was to model watching and reacting as the action unfolded, which is the role of the Chorus, and thus keying the audience into their role as well.

Plays in classical Greece served as important community and religious events beyond mere entertainment in ways that are difficult for modern audiences to imagine. Therefore we ritualized the beginning and ending of the play, effectively "bookending" the production, with fire. At the beginning of the production, the entire royal family, in Greek masks, came out to the foreground of the stage, lit ritual fires in urn-like containers, and then removed their masks. At the end of the play, Ismene, the one character from the royal house left alive, come back to the stage and alone extinguished the blazes and then covered her face with her hands. The members of the Chorus took off their masks, effectively highlighting a reverse mourning technique – instead of veiling the face, the elders reveal their feelings. Doing this en masse ritualized their mourning – and doing this all out of doors, in a Greek-style theater in the daylight, further enhanced the period feel of the play.

I think we accomplished our production goals. The family tree backdrop provided relevant information on relationships; characters were easily identifiable by type; the bifurcation of the Messenger entertained as well as informed; and the Chorus, although its songs were perhaps still somewhat dense in terms of literal meaning, provided movement, song, and spectacle in mood-enhancing and majestic ways. The audience also saw the production in terms of a ritual that could be contextualized in familiar ways – the lighting and extinguishing of a flame. The recognizable device of the mask helped set a Greek-theater tone, as did the outdoor production in the daylight.

Rayor's intention to accurately translate *Antigone* into a play that would be feasible to produce remained foremost in our minds. Greek drama ultimately was meant to *be* produced, and our intention was to turn a classical piece of text into a living piece of theater. Using a live cast to help refine the script and develop a play is a most effective way to achieve this goal.

Happily, the version you see before you works as a dramatic production. The translation combines an accuracy and faithfulness to the original text with an inherent theatricality. The pleasure of collaboration lies in the making of something new. Here, we had the opportunity to work with the translator to take an ancient text and create a piece of theatre that was both fresh and authentic.

Break a leg!

Karen Libman, Professor of Theatre
School of Communications
Grand Valley State University

$\mathcal{N}otes$

**Scene One (*Prologos*: prologue spoken before the entry
of the Chorus)**

(1) Antigone's first speech emphasizes the extreme closeness of the two
sisters, the pervasiveness of their suffering, and her categorization
of people into opposing camps of friends and enemies. The first
line literally reads: "Shared/common self/very-sister/wombmate
head of Ismene" ("head of Ismene" is an endearment). Because
the generational divisions have collapsed in Antigone's family –
her mother is also her father's mother, and so her father is also her
brother – the two sisters have too much in common/shared from
the womb.

(2) The "evils" include their incestuous conception, the suicide of
their mother, Oedipus' curses on himself and his sons, the resulting
war in Thebes, his sons' deaths, and shame on his daughters. The
word translated here as "evils" (*kaka*) is elsewhere "bad things" or
"troubles."

(3) Antigone refers to her sister using the Greek dual form, which
emphasizes her closeness to Ismene: They are a pair, like a pair of
gloves. Antigone uses the dual form again in line 21 for the two of

them, who are linked with their two brothers. Although Ismene, Kreon, and the Chorus use the dual form for the two sisters and the two brothers, Antigone does not speak to her sister in the dual form again after Ismene refuses to help her attempt to bury Polynices.

(4) Disaster: The Greek *atê* means ruin, disaster, doom, blight, or the delusion that causes ruin; it infects people and contaminates their actions. See Padel 1995, pp. 253–5.

(10) The Greek *philos* means friend or kin. Can someone be *philos* and also an enemy? Here Antigone's maternal uncle, the "commander" Kreon, is one of her "enemies."

(15) Polynices' army from Argos was defeated earlier that night.

(18) In fifth-century Athens, respectable women would be expected to remain indoors, and certainly so at night.

(23) Eteokles is the brother who kept the kingship of Thebes and so was the defender against Polynices' attack.

(28–30) It was the family's sacred obligation to provide a proper burial for their dead, which included female lamentation.

(33) Kreon probably first announced his decree on the battlefield that night after defeating the Argives.

(38) Antigone insists that Ismene choose sides; if Ismene were to choose against her, Antigone would consider Ismene *kakê* (evil or base), although from noble stock.

(40) Ismene asks what she could "do or undo" in terms that evoke feminine tasks of fastening or loosening yarn – either weaving or tying a knot in the string of fate.

(49) Greek has a rich vocabulary of laments and vocalizations; *oimoi* (similar to the Yiddish "oy vey") and a sound of disgust, *puh* (323, 1048) are the only ones I left in the translation.

(59) Law: Here *nomos* is Kreon's new decree against burying Polynices. The same word also means "custom": It is the custom (*nomos*) for family members to bury their dead, even though it is the current law (*nomos*) not to bury this particular man.

(73–4) *Philê* (fem.) I will lie with *philos* (masc.). Perhaps this line has erotic/incestuous overtones (see Griffith 2005, pp. 95–6), although it may simply reflect the passion of Antigone's commitment to her dead family members (even while disowning her living relations).

(79) For Ismene, it is impossible (*amêchanos*) to act against the state: Violating civic institutions harms the citizens.

(90) Antigone is in love with the impossible.

(92) Antigone is unfeminine by being active (hunting, burying, desiring).

(93–4) As in line 10, Antigone separates *philos* from enemies; first Kreon is put in the enemy camp, and now Ismene. Why is Antigone committed to her dead brother, but quick to reject her living sister? By setting the brothers against each other in death, Kreon sets the sisters against each other.

(95–6) Ill-conceived plan: Probably sarcastic. Poor planning is a problem for Kreon, too.

(99) The phrase, "You are truly *philos* to your *philoi*," has a double meaning of being committed to kin and dear to them.

Chorus: First Song (*Parodos*: first entrance of the Chorus to the orchestra, which was made through the "side paths" [*par-odos*])
The Chorus remains on stage for the rest of the play. In this chorus in the original Greek, the first and third stanzas (strophe A and antistrophe A) have the same meter; the fifth and seventh stanzas (strophe B and antistrophe B) are also metrically the same. The full Chorus sings these stanzas in unison. In between the strophes and antistrophes are seven-line stanzas with a more regular (anapestic) meter, which are chanted.

The Chorus's mood is in sharp contrast to the opening scene. They rejoice that the dawn after the battle has arrived, with Thebes saved from the defeated Argive army led by Polynices. They also describe how desperate Thebes' situation was, but that Zeus granted them victory, because the invaders were arrogant. Their rejoicing appropriately concludes with a prayer to Thebes' patron god, Dionysos or Bacchus (son of Kadmos' daughter). Dionysos' close (and troubled) relationship with Thebes stems from his premature birth (see line 1116).

(102) Each of the seven gates was successfully defended in a face-off between the leaders of both armies (see 142).

(105) Dirce: a river west of the city.

(111) A Greek pun on Polynices' name, which means "many quarrels."

(112) Polynices is likened here to a ravenous eagle, an odd image because the eagle is Zeus' bird.

(122) Polynices was killed before he could torch Thebes.

(124) Hephaistos and Ares could simply mean fire and war, but using the gods' names evokes their presence in an epic battle.

(126) The serpent or dragon represents Thebes itself because the founder of Thebes, Kadmos, killed the dragon of Ares there. On the advice of Athena, he sowed some dragon's teeth, out of which sprung fully armed men. They immediately killed each other, except the last five, who were the progenitors of the founding families of Thebes (Ovid, *Metamorphoses* 3.32–130).

(132) Zeus struck down Kapaneus, an Argive captain, because of his premature and arrogant boasts of victory.

(134–6) Kapaneus acted as if possessed by Dionysos.

(140) In the Greek image, Ares is the lead horse in a harnessed team; he leads in the destruction of the seven Argive captains.

(144) The Argives left their shields as they fled in defeat, and so they paid Zeus their shields in exchange for their lives.

(145–8) Although Kreon's decree separates the two brothers as friend and enemy of Thebes, the Chorus here emphasizes their sameness.

Scene Two (1st *Epeisodion*: episode between two Choruses; "the addition that gives pleasure")

(162–3) Kreon begins his introductory speech with a ship-of-state metaphor, crediting the gods with setting the state upright again, after tossing it about in the sea of war.

(166) The Chorus of elders "honored the power of the throne," which shows their loyalty to the royal line.

(172) Their hands were "stained" with the *miasma* or pollution of murdering each other.

(173) Kreon's repetition of "power and throne" asserts his right to rule, yet also would sound strongly undemocratic to the Athenian audience. Kreon becomes king through his sister's marriage to Laius and by being the eldest living male related to the house of Laius. His power derives from kinship, even though he repudiates ties to his kin (Polynices here, Antigone, and then Haemon later).

(183) Compare with line 1325.

(182–90) Kreon emphasizes that the state is more important than *philos*; friends are determined by whether they help or harm the state.

(193) Related laws: Kreon's new laws are literally "brothers" to those laws that "strengthen the state."

(222) Greed: Kreon's first use of *kerdos*, "hope of profit," gain.

(243) Terrible: *ta deina* can mean "wondrous, awesome, strange, clever, terrible" and is the same word used in the first line of the following chorus (332).

(253) When the day watchman comes on duty, he sees what the night watch, including this guard, missed. The token burial is done silently, without the noise of tools or wagon, which certainly would have drawn the guards' notice.

(274) Lot: Cast from a shaken helmet.

(294) Bradshaw (1962, p. 209) points out that Kreon is not unreasonable in suspecting bribery and insurrection, because the burial somehow happens under the guards' nose.

Chorus: Second Song (1st *Stasimon*: choral song after entrance song, from the word meaning "stationary")

This is the most famous of all Greek choral songs (echoed in *Hamlet* 2, 2, 303). The song's first three stanzas chart human progress from mastering nature (sea and land), hunting and taming animals, and devising culture (language, laws, and housing). All progress comes from resourcefulness and the use of technology (ships, plows, traps, nets, harnesses, yokes, city policy, and planning). Through clear and creative thinking, people can find their way around the elements, disease, and any other event. Only death remains inescapable. The final stanza introduces the ethical judgments and decisions at the center of communal life. With this song, the Chorus helps frame this particular event in a broader context.

The song follows the report of the mysterious burial and Kreon's first test of character as ruler. The Chorus has in mind the action in the previous scene and may be thinking of Kreon's edict and reaction to the guard. The audience might also see how this song applies to Antigone's extremely resourceful actions: covering her brother in earth, keeping animals at bay, and escaping detection [Mark Beckwith's observation in a 2010 class]. After the song, the guard returns with Antigone in tow and describes the even stranger circumstances of the second burial.

(332) Strange wonders: See note 242.

(349) The Greek *mêchanos* (i.e., machine) is translated as "inventions" here. In line 365, *mêchanos* is translated as "skillful," modifying "technology" (*technê*). The opposite of *mêchanos* is *amêchanos* in line 364: "incurable" (also see line 79).

(359–60) In Greek, the contrasting words *pantoporos, aporos* (all-resourceful, without resources) occur concurrently; I translate

them as "Ingenious" man and "without ingenuity." Likewise in
line 371, the contrasting words *hypsipolis, apolis* (high-city, cityless)
indicate that the law-abiding man has high standing in his city
and that his city is strong, and that lawbreakers are banished and
that their city is weakened.

(369–70) Are the "laws of the land" and the "justice of the gods"
the same thing for the Chorus? Part of the interpretation depends
on which definition of *nomos* (i.e., customs or laws) the Chorus
assumes.

Scene Three (2nd *Epeisodion*)
(376) Antigone is a divine portent or omen of disaster.

(388) Archilochos 122.1 West: referring to an eclipse: Nothing is unex-
pected or sworn impossible, / nothing is amazing since Olympian
Father Zeus / made night out of high noon.... (Rayor 1991,
p. 23)

(397) Unlike the first time, he volunteers to return, because catch-
ing her in the act is a "gift from Hermes," the god of luck and
messengers, among other attributes. (See the *Homeric Hymn to
Hermes*.)

(416) High noon is the Greek witching hour, like our midnight.

(423–5) The Greeks read bird signs as omens, and so Antigone's bird-
like cry is heard as a divine omen appearing out of a divine dust
storm. There will be no new generation for Oedipus' line.

(428) Antigone curses Kreon. Oedipus was also free with curses.
The double burial of Polynices has occasioned much speculation.
Both burials can be explained by human agency alone; we hear

Antigone say she is going to bury her brother, he is discovered buried, and then she is caught in the act the second time. Bradshaw details Antigone's stealth in the dark of night for the first ritual burial, followed by her return under cover of the dust storm to pour (more?) libations. Yet there are also signs of divine assistance to Antigone: She covers Polynices' corpse with dust and leaves without alerting the watchmen or leaving any sign, including footprints, in the dry dust; she also returns to the body through a fierce dust storm that makes the guards close their eyes. Thus she seemingly appears out of the whirlwind, which is itself described as "from heaven" and "divine." (See Scodel 1984a, pp. 55–6.) Both scenes seem to be a mixture of divine portents and human action. Why is there a second burial of Polynices, or why does Antigone return to his body? Assuming Antigone covers him the first time, why does she return to pour libations? Why does she cry aloud instead of remaining silent and then leaving in the dust storm? Even though she cannot "heap up a burial mound" over him (line 81), she performs the ritual actions of covering the body with earth, pouring libations, and mourning aloud. Although the rituals usher the dead into the underworld, the physical body still remains to be disposed of properly to satisfy the living and the gods. She cannot stop the corpse from rotting or keep the dogs and birds from mutilating his body later.

(441) This begins the most famous scene in *Antigone,* in which Antigone and Kreon face off. Kreon's three questions to Antigone give her three opportunities to alter her fate from the punishment of death by stoning. Instead, she cements Kreon's resolution by provoking him. Challenging him publicly on his first day as king, his young niece defies his first laws.

(450) Here Antigone makes clear her alliance to the gods' unwritten, natural laws, the ones of custom, in which it is the family's duty to bury their dead and women's duty to prepare the dead for burial and to lament. It is to the city's benefit not to leave the dead unburied, as the play makes clear. This is also a heavily negative and antagonistic declaration of Antigone's principles in opposition to civil authority.

(451) The goddess Justice (*Dikê*: Right, Order) lives among people and, with the earth goddesses of retribution, the Furies (Erinyes), punish murderers. *Dikê* is the opposite of *hubris*, which is violent action based on an arrogant attitude.

(471) Fierce: raw or savage.

(473) Kreon here states that people too stiff or "stubborn fall hardest"; Haemon makes the same point at lines 712–7.

(480) Here and in line 482, Kreon claims that Antigone acts with arrogance (*hubris*) in first breaking his law and, second, in now boasting about it. When he says she laughs about it, that refers to the heroic ethic of helping friends and harming enemies. The fear is that if one does not punish one's enemies, they will get the last laugh. See line 647.

(487) Every home would have an altar to "Zeus of the courtyard" (Zeus Herkeios), one of the main household deities, which thus can simply mean the family unit. According to Griffith, Kreon is hyperbolic in condemning Antigone even if she were "closer to me by blood than my whole family" (pp. 206–7).

(489) Why does Kreon include Ismene, when Antigone is the one caught in the act? He uses the dual form when referring to the sisters. He distinguishes between the brothers as the good one

and the bad one, but cannot differentiate between the sisters. He interprets Ismene's distress as guilt, at least in the planning of the burial. Yet at lines 561–2 Kreon, although still using the dual form for "girls," clearly sees Antigone as the real troublemaker.

(502) Heroes strive to win glory (*kleos*), which involves doing a deed worthy of fame and having someone tell the story about it afterward.

(503) *Autadelphon*: Antigone uses the exact same word for her brother (self-wombmate/sibling) here as she does in line 1 for Ismene.

(523) Although her brothers died hating each other, she loves them both. The words she uses here are unique in classical Greek for "share in hate" and "share in love."

(527) *Philadelpha*: sister-loving.

(539) Because Ismene is not willing at first to join her in the burial, Antigone rejects her claim to share in the punishment. Here Antigone says, "I didn't share," using the same root word that she uses in addressing Ismene, her "common/shared" sister, in the opening line of the play. Is she trying to protect or reject Ismene? Does she not want to share the punishment or the glory?

(569) The Athenian marriage pledge was for the man to take the woman by the hand (her wrist) "for the plowing of legitimate children."

(570) Literally: "Not so it was as suitable/harmonious for him and for her."

(572) All three lines (572, 574, 576) are assigned to Ismene in the Greek manuscripts. Line 572 is sometimes attributed to Antigone, although it would be highly unusual for a character to interject

a single line into the *stichomythia* (the quick back-and-forth dialogue). If this is Antigone's line, it is the only place where Antigone mentions Haemon specifically. When this line is attributed to Antigone, 574 and 576 are assigned to the Chorus. Yet it is more consistent to have Ismene continue speaking with Kreon until he dismisses the two women to house arrest.

(573) Literally: "your marriage" or "the marriage to which you refer."

(577) Perhaps, according to Kreon, Ismene helps in the decision by aiding Antigone.

(579) Respectable women would stay in the house, not wander outside, like Antigone. This is the first time that Antigone enters the house.

(580) The word for "bold" is the same as "brave" (559).

Third Song (2nd *Stasimon*)

As in the last choral ode, the first strophe and antistrophe have identical meter, as do the second strophe and antistrophe.

The Chorus' reaction to Antigone's capture and Kreon's response in the last scene lead it to focus on the *atê* (see note 5) from the gods that curses Oedipus' family. Yet the Chorus does not blame Antigone or focus on her actions. It sees Antigone's plight as belonging to the family curse; she is truly her father's daughter (471). The Chorus refers explicitly to Antigone's situation. Implicitly, however, the last two paragraphs apply to Kreon, although he is only related to the line of Labdacus (Oedipus' grandfather) by the marriage of his sister into the family. The focus on *atê*, transgression, and deceptive desires introduces Kreon's interaction with his son in the following scene.

(601) Antigone (and Ismene?) is the "last root," which is being cut down by the gods of death.

(603) Fury: A goddess of retribution, usually plural (Erinyes).

(622–5) These lines suggest urgency in and the difficulty of distinguishing evil from good when blinded by divine *atê*. See the previous song (lines 367–8).

(624–5) The repetition of *atê* in the song leads directly to the entrance of Haemon.

Scene Four (3rd *Epeisodion*)

(633) The Chorus and Kreon expect Haemon to speak passionately out of his love and anger for Antigone. Haemon's name means "blood."

(634) Dear: *philos*.

(635) The phrase "when you have" is a circumstantial participle with an ambiguous meaning: if/when/because are all possibilities in English.

(644) The heroic ethic of helping one's friends and harming one's enemies. If one's enemies are not punished or they see you disgraced by your family members, they laugh and so shame you (647).

(663–71) The manuscript has these first four lines (663–6) come after (671), but I accept the transposition based on Griffith's text on the same grounds in terms of sense.

(671) Kreon states that the tyrant must be obeyed in all matters, right or wrong.

(672) *Anarchia* is the opposite of *peitharchia,* "obedience to authority" (676).

(693) Haemon shows no sign of the grief or rage for Antigone that
Kreon and the Chorus expect. He does not express his personal
feelings in his matching reply to Kreon's speech. Instead, by point-
ing out the people's sympathy for Antigone, he tries to move Kreon
from his set path of determining friend or enemy based on obedience to him. According to Haemon, the citizens view Antigone's
actions in heroic terms, as worthy of *kleos* (fame/glory, 695) and
timê (value/honor/respect by the community, 699).

(696) Haemon uses the same word (*autodelphon*) for Antigone's not
leaving her own brother unburied, as Antigone does in line 503.

(711) In referring to Antigone, Kreon says that being too "stubborn"
(stiff/rigid) leads to disaster (473–6).

(715–17) Haemon adds his own ship-of-state metaphor.

(740) Kreon here addresses the Chorus.

(770) Although Kreon seems to give no ground to Haemon, after
the Chorus's two questions he reverses himself on two important
points. First, he acknowledges that Ismene is innocent. This is the
first instance of Kreon accepting the "good counsel" (169) that the
elders, or anyone, have to offer. Second, when the Chorus queries
him about the manner of Antigone's punishment, Kreon changes
the means of her death: Instead of public stoning, she will be sealed
into a cave and left to die. Public stoning relies on a public that
is willing to cast stones; Haemon says the people of Thebes do
not believe she deserves to die for burying her brother; therefore,
Kreon chooses a site removed from the city, which does not require
public participation or provide an opportunity for protest. He can

simply usher her out of sight. By locking her in with some food, he does not actually kill her and so escapes the *miasma* (pollution) of being her murderer. According to Greek thought, her death or rescue is in the gods' hands.

Fourth Song (3rd *Stasimon*)
Because there is no announcement of his departure and reentrance, Kreon probably remains on stage, although he does not speak until line 883. On Haemon's entrance in the last scene, the Chorus and Kreon wonder whether he is maddened with grief over the loss of his "betrothed bride" (628). Even though Haemon presents his case as being motivated by concern for his father, Kreon assumes that Haemon's argument should be dismissed because he is a "woman's slave" (756). In this ode, the Chorus claims that Haemon acts under the influence of Eros (love, passion) for Antigone and so is indeed "mad" (790). Eros and the goddess of love, Aphrodite, are "unbeatable" and so lead human beings astray. These gods are to blame for this quarrel among blood relatives. Although the Chorus comments directly on Haemon's quarrel with his father as deriving from Haemon's love-madness, its language implicates other characters (Kreon, Polynices, Antigone), who also act out of extreme passion.

Scene Five (*Kommos* and 4th *Epeisodion*; *kommos* is from a word meaning "strike or beat one's breast," a dirge or lament in which the Chorus and a character usually sing in alternating stanzas).
The two stanzas of the song lead into the Chorus's announcement of Antigone's entrance. Here, for the first time, the Chorus shows its sympathy for Antigone's plight as she leaves the house for her tomb.

(805) The Chorus and Antigone conflate her death with marriage; her "bridal chamber" is the cave in which she is to be buried alive and thus her tomb. Instead of marrying Haemon, she marries death.

In the *kommos* that follows, the Chorus responds to Antigone's song. Antigone sings in lyric meters until Kreon interrupts (883). After each of Antigone's first two stanzas, the Chorus chants in reply; after her third stanza, it returns to lyric song. When a character sings, it shows high emotion, as it does when the Chorus returns to choral song in an antiphonal exchange with characters. See Helen Bacon (1994/5) for insight on the importance of community in lamentation.

(809) The opening choral song (100) rejoices at the dawn's "Ray of sun" that comes at last after the battle the night before. Here, during this same long day, Antigone bids farewell to her "last light of sun."

(812) Acheron: River of death.

(817–22) The Chorus replies that she chooses death; she is not struck down by disease or violence. Heroes, like Heracles and Odysseus, descend alive to the underworld, and so the Chorus says she is like a hero in gaining glory for her heroic deeds. Unlike those other heroes who descend to Hades and return, however, Antigone is being buried alive and will not return. In addition, the Chorus disapprovingly calls her "*autonomos*" (following her "own law" or being a law unto herself), because she disobeys city laws.

(824–32) Tantalos (a son of Zeus) was king of Sipylus in Lydia (which is often conflated with Phrygia in poetry). The mountain (825), Mt. Sipylus, is in the Tmolos range south of Sardis. Tantalos' daughter, Niobe, was the wife of King Amphion of Thebes and so a "guest" in Thebes. Niobe boasted that she was better than the goddess Leto, because Leto had only two children; in response, Leto's two children (Apollo and Artemis) killed all of Niobe's many children. Niobe returned to Mt. Sipylus, where she was turned to stone, with her tears forming an unending stream flowing over her.

(833) A god turned Niobe into stone, and now Hades puts Antigone to bed for her final rest.

(843) Prosperous men: the Chorus.

(850–2) Earlier, facing death by stoning, Antigone remains steadfast. Locked alive in a cave, however, she is separated from the living and the dead.

(858) The lament for her father's crimes is repeated over and over. The image of the plow also may reflect the incest (a wife plowed by the husband; see line 569). See Michael Clarke (2001).

(868–71) Polynices took an Argive bride. The marriage of her father/brother Oedipus also led to Antigone's death.

(876) In this entire scene, Antigone mentions neither Ismene nor Haemon. She repeats that she has no family grieving for her and that she is the only woman left in her line (882, 941).

(889) By leaving Antigone some food in the cave, Kreon is not technically her murderer and so is "pure" and not stained by *miasma* (see line 770).

(890) She has no home above ground among the living.

(905–12) In her scenes with Ismene and with Kreon, Antigone argues that, according to custom and the laws of the gods, kin must be buried. Here she seems to be arguing that only kin who cannot be replaced (i.e., siblings when the parents are dead) must be buried; replaceable kin (spouse, children) could be left unburied, if the state so decrees. She places the highest value on her natal family. See Sheila Murnaghan (1986) for an insightful article on the relationship of lines 904–20 to the rest of the play, in which Antigone "consistently undervalues human institutions" (p. 200).

(916) In the wedding ritual, a woman's male guardian (*kyrios*) would hand her to the groom, who would take her by the wrist. As Antigone's closest male relative, Kreon would be her *kyrios*. Here, death is the bridegroom.

(925) This: punishment.

(937) Although earlier she violates the city's laws to obey customary practices and the gods' unwritten laws, in her final speech she emphasizes her place in the city.

Fifth Song (4th *Stasimon*)
The Fifth Song emphasizes the power of Destiny (*Moira*) over even those close to the gods. The Chorus refers to three myths, which are roughly connected to either Antigone's situation or Kreon's. Because Kreon is still on stage, perhaps the Chorus feels the need to be oblique. During the Fifth Song, Antigone is locked in the cave. The first two myths refer to people imprisoned – first a woman unjustly confined and then a man justly confined. The third myth (stanzas three and four) also has a woman suffering unjustly.

(944–9) Danaë's father, King Acrisius of Argos, locked her in a bronze room (either underground or in a tower) because of a prophecy that she would bear a son who would kill him. Zeus impregnated her anyway with a shower of gold through the airshaft. When Acrisius discovered the newborn Perseus with Danaë, he enclosed mother and infant in a chest and cast them out to sea. (See Danaë's moving prayer to Zeus for rescue, Simonides PMG 543, Rayor 1991, p. 106.) Eventually, after their rescue and Perseus' slaying of Medusa, Perseus does accidently kill his grandfather.

(955–65) King Lycurgus of the Edonians in Thrace tried to prevent the worship of Dionysos, refusing to recognize him as a god, and was punished with madness and death. (King Pentheus did the same in Thebes.) In this version, Lycurgus violently denied Dionysos and his maenads (possessed female worshippers) and so was imprisoned. There, as his madness faded, he realized his error. In other versions, Lycurgus was blinded by Zeus (*Iliad* 6.130–40), or while driven mad by Dionysos, killed his son – also named Dryas (Apollodorus 3.5.1) or killed both wife and son (*Fabula* 132).

(965) Muses: The nine daughters of Zeus and Mnemosyne ("Memory"), goddesses of inspiration, are frequently portrayed as companions of Dionysos.

(966–87) This tangled myth focuses on the sufferings of Kleopatra, daughter of Boreas (the north wind) and Oreithyia (daughter of Erechtheus, a king of Athens) and her two sons. Kleopatra bore the Thracian king Phineus the two boys (and then died, or was abandoned or imprisoned). Phineus' second wife blinded her stepsons (and Phineus was blinded by Boreas in retribution). Even though Kleopatra was the daughter of a god and royalty, she, and especially her innocent sons, suffered from her bad marriage.

(966–8) The two seas are the Hellespont (by Troy) and the Black Sea. The "Dark Islands" are two tiny islands located near Byzantium, where the Black Sea opens into the Bosporus and Thracian city of Salmydessos. Greeks considered the Thracians barbarians and Thrace home to the god Ares.

(985) Boreas' children, including Kleopatra, had wings.

Scene Six (5th *Epeisodion*)

(988) The blind prophet Tiresias appears in many myths; alive in four extant Greek tragedies, including two other Theban ones (Euripides' *Bacchae* and Sophocles' *Oedipus*); and among the dead in Homer's *Odyssey*.

(993) This may refer to a myth in which Tiresias predicts that Thebes would be saved and Kreon rule if one of his sons died; the Messenger (1302) says that Kreon's wife blames Kreon for the death of his eldest son, Megareus.

(999–1000) Augury is the practice of divination by interpreting bird signs. Tiresias provides a sanctuary or haven for birds so he can have more direct access to their behavior.

(1005–6) When he could not read the bird omens, Tiresias attempts to read the signs through animal sacrifice. Animal sacrifice, a major component in Greek religion, included burning the thigh bones wrapped in fat as an offering to the gods. The organs could be read in divination; the meat provided a communal feast. Here, the gods reject the offerings: Hephaistos represents fire and divine rejection.

(1016–22) Although Antigone completes a ritual burial for Polynices, his mutilated body pollutes the altars and offends the gods. The gods' rejection of Thebes is shown by the unsuccessful sacrifice and unclear omens (1021).

(1038) Electrum: a compound of silver and gold mined near Sardis, the capital of Lydia.

(1040–1) In line 288, when Kreon insists that the gods would not honor his enemies, he claims to understand divine intention (Scodel 1984b, p. 54). Here, he defies Zeus and so endangers Thebes by insisting that Polynices' scattered remains could not defile the gods.

(1060) Kreon's accusations of bribery push Tiresias into revealing a new vision triggered by Kreon's intransigence.

(1080) Enemy states: Argos and her allies, referring to further attacks on Thebes in the mythological tradition. Tiresias' prophecy proves accurate for the loss of Kreon's family; Kreon's actions "will in the future prove to have disastrous results for the city as well" (Roberts 1988, p. 182).

(1100) When Kreon finally is willing to accept advice, the Chorus tells him to unbury the living and bury the dead – in that order.

(1106) As Simonides says, "But with necessity / not even the gods fight" (PMG 542.29–30, Rayor 1991, p. 104).

Sixth Song (5th *Stasimon*)

This follows a traditional hymn formula in invoking Dionysos, asking him to return to his native city from his wanderings (in Italy, Eleusis, and Delphi, etc.), and entreating him to purify Thebes of its sickness. The beat and tone are ecstatic, a bit frenetic, and desperately optimistic that Kreon can rectify his mistakes. The Sixth Song lacks the pure joy and relief found in the matching hymn to Dionysos in the opening chorus.

(1116) When Semele, daughter of Kadmos and the goddess Harmonia, was pregnant with Zeus' son, Hera tricked her into getting

Zeus to reveal himself to her in his true form. As a result, Zeus, in the form of lightning, struck and killed Semele (1139–40). Zeus rescued the premature Dionysos from his mother's womb and sewed him into his own thigh to complete gestation. Thus Dionysos was born twice, once from his human mother and then from his divine father (1149).

(1119–20) Eleusis, a town twenty kilometers northwest of Athens, was the seat of the Eleusinian Mysteries, dedicated to the grain goddess Demeter and her daughter Persephone. Everyone (who could speak Greek, had the price for a sacrificial piglet, and was not a murderer) could be initiated into the Mysteries, which promised initiates prosperity in life and a better afterlife. Demeter's "lap" may mean the rich grain fields around Eleusis.

(1121) Bacchants: Female worshipers of Dionysos, also called maenads.

(1123) Ismenos: A river east of the city.

(1125) Dragon's teeth: See line 126.

(1127–9) The sacred waters of the Kastalian stream flow down from a fissure in a cliff above Delphi, located on Mt. Parnassos (1144) west of Thebes on the Korinthian Gulf. The large Korycian Cave, further up the mountain, was sacred to local nymphs. Although Delphi is best known for Apollo's oracle, Dionysos was worshiped there part of the year.

(1131) Mt. Nysa: Although there were many Nysaean mountains, located in and out of Greece, including in Euboea (the peninsular region east of Thebes, bordering the Aegean), Helen Cullyer (2005) argues persuasively that this is the Thracian Nysa.

(1141) Sickness: Perhaps the physical and religious pollution from Polynices' corpse and the civil strife from Kreon's edict. Or the sickness may refer to the disease of madness in and caused by Antigone, Kreon, and Haemon (Cullyer, 16–17).

(1143) Purifying step: Literally "cathartic foot," which may refer to healing through ecstatic dancing (Scullion 1998).

(1145) Moaning strait: The Euripus, a narrow strait between Euboea and mainland Boeotia. Fierce winds blowing down from Thrace cause the moaning. See "Thracian gales" (585–8) and their connection with *atê*.

(1151) Thyiads: Immortal nymphs accompanying Dionysos, or other female worshipers.

(1154) Dionysos here is literally called "Iakchos," his cult title in the Eleusinian Mysteries. If line 1131 refers to the Thracian Nysa, the Sixth Song evokes "the *full* range of [Dionysos'] activity, from beneficent god of the mystery cults to retributive destroyer in Thrace" (Cullyer, 12; see note 955 on Lycurgus).

Scene Seven (6th *Epeisodion*)

(1155) Amphion was the brother of Kadmos, the founder of Thebes.

(1156) The Messenger's opening speech refers to the uncertainty of human events ("so swift / not even the changing course of a dragonfly"; Simonides 521 PMG, Rayor 1991, p. 101), and that "Without pleasure, / what mortal life is desirable? / what tyrant's power?" (PMG 584.1–3, p. 105).

(1184–5) Eurydice provides a respectable reason for leaving the house.

(1199) Crossroad Goddess: Hecate.

(1200) Plouton: Hades.

(1243) Elise Garrison (1989) argues for Eurydice to begin a slow, silent exit here, while the Chorus and Messenger comment on her silence; she would then enter the *skenê* at line 1252 at the latest.

(1248) In fifth-century Athens, public mourning was restricted. As a respectable wife, Eurydice is expected to begin the antiphonal lamentation inside among other women.

Scene Eight (*Kommos* and *Exodos*: exit "path out")
As in the first *kommos* in Scene Five between Antigone and the Chorus, Kreon's lament is intensified through lyric song. It is striking that Kreon sings, while the Chorus responds in speech. Only in the Chorus's opening (1257–60) and closing (1348–53) statements does it chant. The Chorus's calm, rational tone provides a stark contrast to Kreon's frenzied grief.

(1258) Memorial: Kreon enters carrying Haemon or holding on to Haemon's hand while servants bear him.

(1293) Most likely, servants carry in Eurydice.

(1301) Eurydice kills herself over the altar to Zeus Herkeios in the courtyard (see note 487).

(1303) See line 993. In Euripides' *Phoenician Women*, Kreon's other son is named Menoeceus, not Megareus, and he sacrifices himself to save Thebes after hearing the prophecy that Kreon presses Tiresias to tell in his son's presence.

(1351–2) See line 128: Zeus strikes down boastful men.

Selected Bibliography

Bacon, H. H. 1994/5. The chorus in Greek life and drama. *Arion* 3 (1): 6–24.

Barrett, J. 2002. *Staged narrative: Poetics and the messenger in Greek tragedy*. Berkeley: University of California Press.

Blundell, M. W. 1989. *Helping friends and harming enemies: A study in Sophocles and Greek ethics*. Cambridge: Cambridge University Press.

Bradshaw, A. T. von S. 1962. The watchman scenes in the *Antigone*. *Classical Quarterly* 12 (2): 200–11.

Bushnell, R. W. 1988. *Prophesying tragedy: Sign and voice in Sophocles' Theban plays*. Ithaca: Cornell University Press.

Csapo, E. and W. J. Slater. 1995. *The context of ancient drama*. Ann Arbor: University of Michigan Press.

Clarke, M. 2001. Thrice-ploughed woe (Sophocles, *Antigone* 859). *Classical Quarterly* 51 (2): 368–73.

Cropp, M. 1997. Antigone's final speech (Sophocles, *Antigone* 891–928). *Greece & Rome* 44 (2): 137–60.

Cullyer, H. 2005. A wind that blows from Thrace: Dionysus in the fifth stasimon of Sophocles' "*Antigone*." *Classical World* 99 (1): 3–20.

Demand, N. H. 1994. *Birth, death, and motherhood in classical Greece.* Baltimore: Johns Hopkins University Press.

Didaskalia. http://www.didaskalia.net.

Foley, H. P. 2001. *Female acts in Greek tragedy.* Princeton: Princeton University Press.

Garrison, E. 1989. Eurydice's final exit to suicide in the *"Antigone." Classical World* 82 (6) 431–5.

Goldhill, S. 2007. *How to stage Greek tragedy today.* Chicago: University of Chicago Press.

Griffith, M., ed. 1999. *Sophocles: Antigone.* Cambridge Greek and Latin Classics. Cambridge: University of Cambridge Press. [Greek edition, with excellent introduction and commentary.]

———. 2005. The subject of desire in Sophocles' *Antigone.* In *The soul of tragedy: Essays on Athenian drama.* Eds., V. Pedrick and S. M. Oberhelman, 91–135. Chicago: University of Chicago Press.

Holt, P. 1999. Polis and tragedy in the *"Antigone." Mnemosyne* 52 (6): 658–90.

Kirkwood, G. M. 1994. *A study of Sophoclean drama.* Ithaca: Cornell University Press.

Knox, B. M. W. 1964. *The heroic temper. Studies in Sophoclean tragedy.* Berkeley: University of California Press.

Lawler, L. B. 1964. *The dance in ancient Greece.* Middletown, CT: Wesleyan University Press.

Ley, G. 2006. *A short introduction to the ancient Greek theater.* Revised ed. Chicago: University of Chicago Press.

Mackay, E. A. 1989. Fugard's *The Island* and Sophocles' *Antigone* within the parameters of South African protest literature. In *Literature and revolution.* Ed. D. Bevan, 145–62. Amsterdam: Editions Rodopi.

Morwood, J. 1993. The double time scheme in *Antigone*. *Classical Quarterly* 43 (1): 320–1.

Murnaghan, S. 1986. *Antigone* 904–920 and the institution of marriage. *American Journal of Philology* 107 (2): 192–207.

Nelli, M. F. 2009. Identity, dignity and memory: Performing/rewriting *Antigone* in post-1976 Argentina. *New Voices in Classical Reception Studies* 4: 70–82.

Neuburg, M. 1990. How like a woman: Antigone's 'inconsistency.' *Classical Quarterly* 40 (1): 54–76.

Padel, R. 1995. *Whom gods destroy*. Princeton: Princeton University Press.

Rayor, D. J. 1991. *Sappho's lyre: Archaic lyric and women poets of ancient Greece*. Berkeley: University of California Press.

———. 2004. *The Homeric hymns*. Berkeley: University of California Press.

Rehm, R. 1992. *Greek tragic theatre*. London: Routledge.

———. 1994. *Marriage to death: The conflation of wedding and funeral rituals in Greek tragedy*. Princeton: Princeton University Press.

Roberts, D. H. 1988. Sophoclean endings: another story. *Arethusa* 21 (2) 177–96.

Scodel, R. 1984a. Epic doublets and Polynices' two burials. *Transactions of the American Philological Association* 114: 49–58.

———. 1984b. *Sophocles*. Boston: Twayne Publishers.

———. 2005. Sophoclean tragedy. In *A companion to Greek tragedy*. Ed. J. Gregory, 233–50. Malden, MA: Blackwell Publishing.

Scullion, S. 1998. Dionysos and *katharsis* in "*Antigone*." *Classical Antiquity* 17 (1): 96–122.

Segal, C. 1981. *Tragedy and civilization: An interpretation of Sophocles.* Cambridge, MA: Harvard University Press.

————. 1995. *Sophocles' tragic world: Divinity, nature, society.* Cambridge, MA: Harvard University Press.

Steiner, G. 1986. *Antigones.* Oxford: Oxford University Press.

Taplin, O. 2003. *Greek tragedy in action.* 2nd ed. London: Routledge.

Tyrrell, W. B. and L. J. Bennett. 1998. *Recapturing Sophocles' Antigone.* Lanham, MD: Rowman & Littlefield Publishers.

Walton, J. M. 2006. *Found in translation: Greek drama in English.* Cambridge: Cambridge University Press.

Wiles, D. 1997. *Tragedy in Athens: Performance space and theatrical meaning.* Cambridge: Cambridge University Press.

————. 2000. *Greek theatre performance.* Cambridge: Cambridge University Press.

Winnington-Ingram, R. P. 1980. *Sophocles: An interpretation.* Cambridge: Cambridge University Press.

Zeitlin, F. 1990. Thebes: Theater of self and society in Athenian drama. In *Nothing to do with Dionysus?* Eds. J. Winkler and F. Zeitlin, 130–67. Princeton: Princeton University Press.

CPSIA information can be obtained
at www.ICGtesting.com
Printed in the USA
LVOW03s0744180817

545219LV00001B/3/P